FOREWARNING

This book is written entirely from a female point of view. It has been produced by a woman, with other women.

I recognise, of course, that women can be difficult too, and that relationships look different from a man's perspective. But that is not the concern of this book.

DIFFICULT MEN

ARABELLA MELVILLE

VERMILION
London

1 3 5 7 9 10 8 6 4 2

Text copyright © Arabella Melville 1998

First published in the United Kingdom in 1999 by Vermilion
an imprint of Ebury Press
Random House,
20 Vauxhall Bridge Road,
London SW1V 2SA

Random House Australia (Pty) Limited
20 Alfred Street, Milsons Point, Sydney,
New South Wales 2061, Australia

Random House New Zealand Limited
18 Poland Road, Glenfield,
Auckland 10, New Zealand

Random House South Africa (Pty) Limited
Endulini, 5A Jubilee Road,
Parktown 2193, South Africa

Random House UK Limited Reg. No. 954009

A CIP catalogue record for this book is available from the British Library

ISBN: 0 74 932244 6

Printed and bound in Great Britain by
Creative Print and Design Wales, Ebbw Vale

CONTENTS

ACKNOWLEDGEMENTS

This book could not have been written without the help of the women whose stories appear in its pages. I thank them most sincerely for their courage in sharing their experiences and the lessons they learnt with me and through me, with others. I also want to thank all those who contributed by putting me in touch with their friends or encouraging women to contact me. I am grateful, also, to the journalists who agreed to run stories in their papers, and the producers who gave me opportunities to appeal for volunteers by speaking about this book on local radio.

I should like to acknowledge my debt to those who helped me to understand the nature of violence and its antecedents, and who encouraged me to believe that the problem could be overcome: in particular, Charleen Agostini and Bob and Sue Johnson.

I should like to thank my agent for his help and my publishers both for their faith in this book and for patience that went beyond anything I could reasonably expect. I am especially grateful to my editor, Jacqueline Burns for her care and thoughtfulness.

Finally, I must acknowledge the contribution of my partner, Colin Johnson. We spent many hours discussing this book and my thinking is inevitably influenced by his. Although he is the inspiration for this book, I disagree with his assertion that he must be the most difficult man anyone is likely to encounter. Colin has shown great courage by demonstrating by example that men can change. My admiration for his intellect and integrity continues to deepen over the decades of our relationship.

PART ONE

THE CURSE OF TRUE LOVE

CHAPTER 1

A DIFFICULT PROBLEM

Are men difficult? Women always smile when I tell them the title of this book. They know precisely what I'm talking about. They may be uncertain about *how* difficult their *own* partners really are – many are eager to make it clear that their men, as individuals, aren't *all that bad*, by comparison with some they hear about – but basically, we agree. Men, as a group, are *difficult*. Behaving badly comes naturally to most of them. They may put on a good act at work and in public, but women know a different reality in the home.

Despite the fact that women know that living with men can be challenging, most choose to do it. We feel that the advantages usually outweigh the difficulties. We may believe that we'll be able to tame the man, control the worst excesses of his behaviour sufficiently to make him an acceptable companion. And we're liable to be irrationally biased by love, so that a gamble that friends warn is crazy can seem worth taking.

Then we try to live for the rest of our lives with the consequences of that choice. Most women value their relationships and do their best to make them work, but when they're dealing with particularly difficult men, it can be very hard to know what to do.

This book describes how women can succeed in relationships with such men. It shows how some women do manage to change the man's behaviour and eliminate major problems that affect them both. Those who can't change their relationships as much as they'd like, tell how they find ways to enjoy their lives despite acknowledged problems. These first-hand accounts provide signposts to effective ways of dealing with common difficulties that women experience when they live with men they love.

This is not an objective, academic book, nor a work of psychology, sociology or anthropology. It is a search for personal, subjective reality which women will recognise.

Abuse emotional and/or physical – was the most common type of problem that women brought to me. There were other women with these experiences whose stories, for one reason or another, I was unable to record. Even though I was not specifically looking for women who had experienced these sorts of abuse, they became the dominant themes in this book: a curious twist in the story of the book itself, which I shall tell in the next few chapters.

Although I had not intended to focus on violence, I was particularly interested in it. This was partly because of my personal experience, but also because domestic violence is widely regarded as an intractable problem. The book reveals how this problem can be solved, and men can cease to be violent if the woman changes the way she behaves. Other contributors describe a range of problems, from infidelity to drug abuse. Each woman has found an individual way of changing her relationship with her own difficult man.

While I believe that we can learn from the experience of other women, this is not a book of instructions that purports to show how to transform any abusive relationship into a dream partnership. I do not imagine that this is possible in every case; indeed, it may be very seldom that a woman caught up in an abusive partnership can stop the abuse and make the relationship work. Maybe the majority of women who live with difficult men would be better off without them. I cannot say, and I do not believe that anyone knows for sure. But none of the women who contributed to this book *wanted* to leave their men, so they dealt with the problem in the most effective ways they could find.

Transforming a relationship is not easy, and many women might be unable or unwilling to go to the same lengths as some of those whose stories appear in this book. However, I believe that there are benefits for those women who do persevere and succeed: they learn about themselves. Even if, in the end, they decide not to stay with the man, the experience of acting within a difficult relationship to make it work better will make them stronger and more resilient.

This picture of difficult men and virtuous women probably seems sexist. Well, I do not pretend that this is a balanced or objective book. It is concerned purely with the woman's point of view: it was written by a women on the basis of conversations with other women. Men were the objects, not the subjects, of these conversations. I began this work with the conviction that women can find men so different from themselves (in the context of the home, at least) that often, they might as well be aliens. It's about how two fundamentally different creatures manage to live together.

I used to think, when I was in my late teens and early twenties, that men and women were basically identical in their emotional and mental makeup. All that really differed, I imagined, were the genital organs and secondary sexual characteristics – breasts, distribution of body hair, that sort of thing. Any other differences, I felt sure, were due to social conditioning and patriarchal attitudes.

At that stage in my life, I was rebelling against my mother and all I thought she stood for – particularly the view of women as weak, over-emotional beings. I saw myself as a feminist and rational scientist; the distorting glasses of my idealism were at their strongest. I would have rejected the sort of statements I made in previous paragraphs as heresy.

Ironically, I was married at the time to a man who bullied and belittled me while proclaiming his belief in sexual equality. I used to make his tea and darn his socks and struggle to make myself into the sort of woman I believed he wanted me to be. As I said, my distorting glasses were very strong then.

Then I started living in the real world, outside the safe confines of universities and exclusive discussions among the intelligensia. My views slowly began to change. Most of all, they changed through my observation of animals, coloured by the effects of years of academic training in behavioural psychology.

I saw farm animals behaving in ways that I had previously believed were purely the results of human socialisation. I watched my cockerel offering his hens gifts of succulent morsels of food and standing back proudly as the ladies shared them, just as a man might court women with chocolates. (In fact, it was likely to be a piece of my partner's cream doughnut or a small wriggling frog.) He acted like the perfect gentleman – at least until he wanted sex, when he appeared as insensitive to the hens' feelings as the most macho male.

I was impressed both by the differences between male and female behaviour in every species I watched and, at the same time, by the similarities in gender-specific behaviour across different species. Whether the animal was a sheep, a chicken or a cat, its social behaviour was often surprisingly similar to that of a human of the same sex – and quite different from that of an opposite-sex member of its own species.

Eventually I came to realise how fundamentally different men and women are, and extensive reading over the years strengthened that conviction. Much research evidence shows that socially sensitive behaviour is inherited by women, and therefore develops naturally, whereas it has to be learnt by men, reveals part of the psycho-biological basis of these differences. No doubt continued research into sexual dimorphism in brain function and behaviour will uncover other aspects.

In view of these differences, it is perhaps predictable that there is friction when men and women try to live together. Women find men difficult to deal with (and – yes, I admit it – men can find women difficult) because of these basic differences. It is no coincidence that teams which function most smoothly as units are almost always single sex. Their members understand each other better, there's less ambiguity in communication, they tend to react in more similar ways in the context of the group.*

One reason why women will always tend to find men difficult, and vice versa, is this: the response that a certain pattern of behaviour would produce among members of their own sex is different from the reaction it elicits from the opposite sex. Misjudgements, misunderstandings and misinterpretations are

* See Deborah Tannen's books, particularly *You Just Don't Understand: Women and Men in Conversation* (Virago, 1991) for illustration of this point.

common. In addition, some deep-seated differences of attitude between the sexes are probably biologically determined. The clash between the woman's tendency to value consensus and co-operation and the man's impulse to compete and dominate is well-documented and particularly likely to cause difficulties in their mutual relationship.

Because a woman wouldn't react the same way as a man, we sometimes fail to predict how men will see things or understand why they react as they do. It's hard to live with them when you sometimes can't deal with them. Making such relationships work requires that we learn to understand how what we do is perceived by men, and how our actions affect them. Women often try to understand by imagining how they would react were they in the other person's place, but with men this may not work. Equally, men are frequently mystified by the way women react. So both groups make mistakes about the anticipated consequences of their actions.

The biological basis of gender differences does not imply, however, that we can't bridge the gaps. We all have the ability to learn new forms of social interaction, and one context in which this learning occurs is the long-term partnership between woman and man. We may learn appropriate, effective and mutually satisfying ways of interacting, or – often building on previous maladaptive learning – we may develop interaction patterns that have undesirable consequences.

What one partner does in a relationship inevitably affects the way the other behaves. But members of both sexes are prone to think that the other's reaction arises spontaneously from within him or her, rather than as a result of the interaction between them. So we tend to blame each other for problems and label each other in unhelpful and antagonistic ways, such as neurotic, inconsistent, nagging or aggressive. Blaming and labelling your partner can mean you avoid considering the possibility that you may play a part in provoking the reaction you condemn.

Both men and women learn and adapt in social situations, usually without being aware of what they're learning or how the situation leads them to learn new ways of behaving. Sometimes, unintentionally, we learn patterns of behaviour that create or exacerbate problems in relationships; harmful patterns of behaviour develop through damaging forms of interaction between partners. It may be possible to solve problems by identifying these damaging patterns and replacing them with behaviour that is likely to improve the relationship.

The message of this book is that change is always possible. The stories it contains show how women in any walk of life can change their own behaviour and, by so doing, change the way they relate to the men in their lives. This inevitably changes the way their men relate to them. We can all become set in habitual ways of acting and reacting, but we can change if we are motivated to do so, and we do change in response to changing circumstances.

Change will occur because it takes two to play any particular game in a relationship. What you are effectively doing is saying 'I'm not playing the bad games, the ones I don't like, any more; I'm going to play the good games, the ones we can both enjoy. And I'm encouraging you to join me.'

From the point of view of this book – a partisan, yet practical, point of view – the genesis of the man's difficult behaviour does not matter. I am interested in the ways women solve the problems. What was important to me when I collected accounts of life with difficult men, was that although the women had found them difficult they had discovered some way to deal with that which allowed the partnership to survive.

This book is about the way women decide how they will behave in relationships – not about the relationships themselves, nor even, really, the men. It is concerned with women, their feelings, their experiences, their personal ways of interacting with the world, and especially that corner of the world that they share with a man. My aim in writing it was to offer readers the opportunity to learn from the experience of women who live with, and love, difficult men. Some have been through hell in their relationships, but each volunteered to talk openly about the way she dealt with her situation, and the reasons she chose to stay with her partner.

CHAPTER 2
SUBJECTIVE TRUTH: OBJECTIVE REALITY

The women whose voices I recorded for this book talk about their situations from their own points of view. It begins with my journey and the experiences that led to the creation of the book. Everybody I know agrees that my long-term partner, Colin, is an *exceptionally* (his italics) difficult man for anyone to live with. I have been well aware of that for almost a quarter of a century, yet I do not believe I shall ever leave him. I have learnt a great deal through living with him, including how to act to minimise problems with facets of his personality and behaviour that used to cause me great distress.

When Colin and I began to talk publicly about solving problems we've had over the years, some people suggested that what might work for us could not be expected to work for others. I recall, particularly, the occasion when we were guests on *This Morning* with Richard and Judy. After the first part of the programme, we were chatting with the programme's agony aunt, Denise Robertson, a wise and perceptive woman. 'It's all very well for you,' she said. 'You are middle-class, educated intellectuals. It's different for people who don't have your intellect or your privileges. Your solutions won't work for them.' And indeed, the deeply distressing phone-in later that morning, when woman after woman told how she had suffered at the hands of her husband, seemed to suggest she was right.

But I was convinced that what I had learnt did have potential value for many other women. None of those who had rung the programme had actually tried to solve the problem in the same way as I had; all had tried to placate their husbands in the hope that this would make them behave better. That certainly doesn't work.

I was talking about a completely different type of solution, one where women decide for themselves what they will do rather than accept things as they are, and thus empower themselves within the relationship. I knew that women did not have to be victims: they could take control.

Although I felt sure that a woman did not need to be an educated intellectual to learn to deal with these problems effectively, I also recognised that answers were not easy to find. After all, I, with a doctorate in psychology problem-solving ability and experience of counselling, had found it very impossible to solve these problems without help. But if I could show that women of varied types and backgrounds had also worked out how to manage difficult men, this might reveal that there were general solutions to problems of this kind, which were available to all women. It would then be harder for my critics to dismiss what these women, collectively, were saying.

In the course of my research, I talked with some truly wonderful women whose achievements I found awe-inspiring – although they would probably be amazed to be described in such terms. Others are still struggling – coping with, rather than managing, their relationships – yet they are surviving and feel that they continue to make progress. I did not seek accounts from women who are clearly victims of difficult men; while we should acknowledge the cruelty of which human beings are capable, I see no benefit in dwelling on this unless we can make progress towards effective solutions.

The interviews reveal many common features in the ways that women deal with problems of this sort. The final part of the book brings these together, drawing out recurring themes and lessons. Women who love difficult men can, by applying this knowledge, gain access to the power to make their relationships more rewarding.

PART TWO

LIFTING MY CURSE

CHAPTER 3

A SECRET, DISCOVERED

The story of this book begins with a train journey from my home in West Wales to London, where I had an appointment with the features editor of *Cosmopolitan*. For many years, I had made part of my living from journalism, taking advantage of my academic background in psychology by writing about emotions and behaviour. As the train rattled along the silver Towy estuary that misty summer morning, I was mulling over an idea for an article on how women can love some aspects of men and hate others, and how we reconcile the pleasure with the pain.

I knew it was a complex issue and I believed that many aspects of it had not been discussed sufficiently. It's too easy to classify relationships as good or bad, acceptable or unacceptable, brushing over the reality that they are a patchwork of both. The balance changes from time to time; qualities that appeal in some situations can become a real drag in others, and features that don't seem important early in the relationship can turn into major problems later on. Some desires are in conflict with others and people are not consistent in their expectations. To make matters worse, what you think you are getting may turn out to be something different, what you think you really want may just not be available, or you may find there is an unacceptable price to pay. There are a lot of intertwining issues, each of which may change with time and circumstances.

And what if we change partners, only to meet the same problems in successive relationships? This is a very common pattern. Could it be that we choose difficult men, perhaps not intentionally, but because their difficult behaviour is, at some level, bound up with what attracts us, or what we need? To what degree do women play a part in creating the man with whom they live – whether saint or villain? Do some women actively elicit men's unacceptable features, presumably without realising what they're doing?

Like many ideas of this sort, this one was based on my own experience. My own twenty-year relationship with Colin had always been a mixture of extremes, wonderful and dreadful by turn. The paradox of loving and resenting my partner was all too familiar.

Sitting around a table in the colourful and busy *Cosmo* open-plan office with two editors, I explained the essence of the article I wanted to write. But soon it became clear that they were not about to buy the sort of general notions I was offering. They wanted specifics.

What, one of them asked, was the biggest problem I'd actually experienced with my partner? What made *my* man especially difficult to live with?

They both looked at me expectantly.

This caught me outside my rehearsed routines of thought. I had been considering relationship patterns in a general sort of way, not specific issues within my own. I hesitated, then told them the truth. Yes, Colin was difficult. The hardest thing had been his aggression towards me: it had almost driven me away. But I had learnt how to manage it.

Their eyes lit up. This was something they wanted to hear about. More details, please! Had I actually experienced violence? Had Colin hit me?

Had I been less naïve, I would probably have refused to be drawn. But I find it very hard not to answer direct questions truthfully and I rarely notice circling vultures.

'Yes,' I told them quietly.

Their eyebrows rose in anticipation. 'Yes,' I continued, 'Colin has hit me. Not often, but enough for me to become afraid of him. That really undermined our relationship. The fear is there so much of the time, you are always on your guard, always nervous, when you live with a violent man.' The memory of my past was still sufficiently recent to chill me slightly.

Smiling reassuringly, they poured more tea. The tone became conciliatory. 'Do you have any scars?'

'Only a little one,' I responded, holding out my hand to show them the damage to my little finger. 'But he doesn't hit me any more. All that has stopped,' I emphasised, 'because I learnt how to prevent it. I'm not afraid of him now.' Despite what I was saying, I felt I was on the defensive.

They smiled and held a short whispered conference. Then I got my commission: an article on living with violence. It wasn't at all what I had intended to write.

Returning home, I confronted the realisation that I had agreed to something I hadn't even considered, let alone thought through. It was the most disturbing commission I had ever accepted. Until that day, I'd only discussed Colin's violence with my counsellor. Now, I was planning to share this unhappy experience with the world.

I was convinced I did have something important to say on the subject: after all, I had stopped his violence and I thought I could explain how. I felt certain that my problem was in the past, but that my experience of solving it could be helpful to other women who confront aggressive and even violent men. For all that, I had serious misgivings. I felt that to expose Colin as a 'wife-beater' would be too cruel. I also felt anxious about exposing myself as someone who had put up with that sort of abuse: perhaps irrationally, I was ashamed. So, for the first time in my life, I decided to write anonymously.

At home on our Welsh smallholding, I told Colin what had happened. That I had agreed to write this article. I was nervous, not knowing how he would feel. This wasn't something we had discussed.

He was completely calm, unruffled. Then, to my astonishment, he questioned my decision that the piece should be anonymous. Obviously, he knew how much I valued my integrity; he often accused me of 'writing from the missionary position' in my obsessive pursuit of the truth at any cost to myself. Would what I was going to write be honest and factual? Of course. Would not this article contain a message that could be of great value to many women? I believed it would. (He can be just like a lawyer at times.) Would the article hurt or embarrass any uninvolved third party? It would not. Then, the crucial personal question. Would there be unbearable embarrassment or shame for me? I thought for some time before deciding that actually, I could live with this sort of exposure, and the piece would be more powerful if I did put my name on it. I would stand behind this, as I had stood behind controversial articles before.

All that mattered to Colin was that the piece should be honest. He is a philosopher; what is important to him is that things should be as accurate as they can be.

I didn't look forward to writing it. I would have to go over ugly experiences and relive the distress I'd felt at the time. I'd have to re-create past pain and anger before I could experience the relief of having shed it from my life once more. Only in this way would I be able to clarify in my own mind precisely how the violence had been stopped, and how I had lost my fear of Colin.

I had begun work on the most controversial article of my writing career.

CHAPTER 4

SYNTHESIS

An unforgettable session with Charleen, a counsellor specialising in psychosynthesis, marked the beginning of the end of Colin's violence towards me.

I had arrived in a very distressed state. At that time, Colin and I had a small farm, and we had been trimming the sheep's hooves that day. It's an unpleasant job, physically demanding and emotionally stressful, but essential to the animals' welfare.

Every time we did this job, Colin would get frustrated and irritated and take his bad temper out on me. Even before the real work began, he'd criticise the preparations I made, complaining that I didn't tie knots correctly, or that I hadn't put the footbath in the right place, or something – there was always something. Then, when we had kicking, protesting sheep to catch, turn and treat, when our hands were bleeding and our legs bruised, he would rage and shout and lash out at the sheep and me. And I would end up in tears.

Seeing me so upset, Charleen wanted to know what had been going on. My explanation led to a general discussion about Colin's violent outbursts. This, Charleen recognised, was what we needed to work on.

I had always seen Colin's violence as his problem. I'd often wished he'd seek help – and told him so – but he had always refused because he considered the problem lay in our situation or my inability to do things properly, and that he did not need the sort of help that a therapist might offer. So I thought there was nothing I could do about it, apart from leave him. I'd considered that often, but decided against it: I was trying to make the relationship work, I didn't want to give up on it or him. Nobody knew about the violence, it wasn't something I cared to talk about. And it wasn't obvious; I didn't get thumped frequently and Colin hadn't caused any serious damage – except to our relationship.

But his violence was a serious problem for me. Every time he got angry, I was afraid of what he might do. I felt scared whenever he raised his voice. I was afraid to talk to him about some things, in case he would get angry.

Charleen decided that we should use role-playing to clarify precisely what went on when Colin became angry. I acted my part while she played Colin. Fortunately, she knew him well enough to be able to imitate his behaviour remarkably well – even though she'd never seen him angry.

She was so convincing when she stood over me and shouted that I reacted exactly as I did when Colin attacked me. I cringed and curled into a ball, trying to protect my face with my arms. I became incoherent, unable to speak. She harangued me, demanding that I explain why I was behaving in such a stupid manner and telling me how useless I was. I couldn't answer, I could barely stammer. There was an immovable lump in my throat. Tears streamed down my face.

Then Charleen reverted to her own identity and I became calm again. After a short period of recovery time, we swapped roles. I acted Colin, trying to experience the mixture of frustration, irritation and incomprehension that he expressed when there was a job to do and I was failing to cope. I stood and vented my rage on the hapless Charleen, who cried and cringed as I had done. And I found myself feeling increasingly furious, even wanting to hit this miserable creature in front of me.

When we talked about what had been happening, it was a revelation. For the first time, I began to understand how the cringing victim elicits aggression.

This is how I came to see the aggressor's perspective: *You're already feeling frustrated. You're pissed off, you're on a short fuse. You can't get through to her, she's blocking you with her emotional state. She's making things worse when you want her to make things better. She becomes the source of the problem. You go over the edge, you can't see any option but to hit her. In a strange way, hitting her makes you feel better. It burns off some of the adrenalin, releases some of the tension.* I could also see that if hitting someone meant that the aggressor felt better, that would tend to reinforce the behaviour.

I saw how my defensiveness made it impossible for us to communicate in an adult manner. I realised how, in situations where Colin tended to become aggressive, my fear made him more so. I understood how his frustration increased when I blocked his attempts to communicate, until he would feel that the only way he could get a reaction was by violence. I saw how completely I prevented communication by my inability to talk, by hiding my face, by crying.

At no point did Charleen suggest that I was to blame for any of this. The crucial point was that my behaviour – of not standing up for myself and allowing myself to be bullied – made Colin's violence more probable. So it might be possible, I realised, to reduce the probability of violence by behaving differently.

I couldn't, of course, change the way I reacted just like that. It is not enough only to see what is going wrong; I had to understand it and learn a new way to react.

Charleen's next step was to gently encourage me to return to my experience of that state of fear. She told me to imagine the physical sensations – the pain in my diaphragm, the tightness in my neck, the sense of pressure in my head. Closing my eyes, I re-experienced these all too familiar feelings. Then she asked me if I could remember when I first felt that way. A picture formed in my mind; I recalled a bullying teacher at my first school, who used to whack me across the knuckles because I couldn't read and because I drew pictures in my exercise book. I was terrified of him. Next, I remembered my older half-brother, cold and cruel in the kitchen. He used to smack my legs so they really stung. I was scared of him, too.

Men had frightened me when I was a child, and that frightened child was still there, deep in my psyche. I realised that I wasn't reacting to Colin's aggressiveness as an adult partner would: I was behaving as someone who could not avoid the punishment, *someone with no power*. I was reverting to the child, dumbstruck with fear.

My immediate response to this revelation was to be angry with myself. How stupid I was – I should know better than to act like a child! But Charleen would have none of that. The judgemental part of my mind, she pointed out, was reacting just like Colin – and colluding with him.

She asked me how I would behave if this were a child I knew, another frightened child, not me. I said I would comfort, protect and encourage her. Charleen suggested that I should treat this part of myself as well as I would treat any other child. And, accepting the logic of her advice, I began to forgive myself for my weakness. Slowly, I started to feel stronger.

Realising that Colin's behaviour was cueing childhood memories, I came to see the whole situation differently. By telling myself that I was an adult, not a powerless child facing a bullying teacher, I found I could separate illusion from reality. When I concentrated on dealing with the present, not the emotional residue of the past, the fear faded. Instead of panicking and cringing, I began to stand up to Colin.

When I learnt to treat Colin as an equal rather than as someone who had power over me, he became less prone to try to bully, belittle, and intimidate me. I was able to see that his behaviour was unacceptable, and to tell him so. Slowly, as I learnt to identify and change more facets of my victim behaviour, my whole relationship with Colin began to change.

I understood, now, that my reaction to his aggression was a conditioned emotional response – something that I had studied in my research in psychology, but which I had failed to relate to my own experience at home. It is an emotional reaction far in excess of what is appropriate to the situation, learnt when an individual is punished and has no way to escape. Cues associated with the punishment lead to a strong emotional reaction that can distort behaviour dramatically, and can prevent the victim from learning how to cope even when new opportunities arise – a state called conditioned helplessness. Colin's accusations and raised voice were triggering a reaction that was rooted in my childhood experience.

My behaviour – which was an expression of that emotional reaction – contributed to the problem. For example, I was avoiding Colin's eyes. People who feel they are equal will look directly at each other. Subordinates and those who feel embarrassed, ashamed or guilty look away. Because cueing those childhood memories had made me react as a child, I was not behaving as Colin's equal. To remedy this, I decided that I would take a deep breath (which would help to keep me calm) and make myself continue to look at him when he started to raise his voice.

When I understood that I was in a position to change the way we interacted, I was no longer overwhelmed by fear. I still felt nervous, but I was determined to stand up for myself. And I realised that if I did so, this could have a cascade of other effects which would alter the whole sequence of events.

My long-term interest in behavioural psychology and animal behaviour set me thinking about the way animals deal with potential aggressors. If a cat shows fear when she meets a dog, if she turns tail and runs, she gets chased; but if she faces the dog without fear, she is not harmed.

The same is true of sheep and dogs. A good sheepdog stares at the ewes to gain control. He can move a whole flock where he wishes, by intimidating them with his 'eye'. But this only works if the sheep feel and show fear. On our farm, we had a small ewe who did not fear the dog; she would turn and face him, look him in the eye and challenge him by stamping her delicate foot. When this ewe had a lamb to protect, she would chase dogs away. We called her Dog-death and treated her with respect.

Ewes and cats who face down dogs do not succeed because they are large or strong or even particularly clever. They do not get bullied because they look right back at the bully and refuse to be intimidated. I was learning to do that too.

I had colluded with Colin's behaviour by accepting it. In some way, I felt I deserved abuse. He would point out how I'd failed and I would accept his judgement and feel inadequate. But now I saw that abuse is not appropriate, whatever the circumstances; any error I might have made was irrelevant. Punishment for what may be seen as an error is never justified.

I made a decision to refuse, in future, to tolerate abuse. I told him straight that abuse of any form was unjustifiable, unacceptable, and must stop if he wanted a continuing relationship with me. I resolved that if he started to raise his voice, I would tell him firmly that I would not stay to be shouted at. If we had something to discuss, we should do it without raising our voices. If he wouldn't talk to me in a tone of voice that I found acceptable and non-threatening, I would walk away. And that was precisely what I started to do, every time he began to raise his voice or insult me.

Soon, Colin became involved in this process of creating change. He wasn't happy with the sort of relationship we had, though he seemed unable to change his behaviour. He didn't want me to fear him. What he really wanted was an adult partner, someone he would not be tempted to bully. My tendency to revert to a frightened child had long been a source of irritation to him.

I continued to work through these issues with Charleen. Every time I returned from a therapy session it sparked off long discussions with Colin, when we went through what I'd learnt and the implications for both of us. And when he understood better why I reacted the way I did, his judgement of me became less harsh.

It was important for both of us to recognise the destructive synergy of our reactions. He told me he hadn't realised that I was so afraid, he didn't know that what he saw as insignificant acts had such a great impact on me. He was always astonished at how easily I became bruised; astonished, too, at the psychological pain I suffered. He didn't always remember hitting me: it was as though he wasn't properly conscious of his actions. And he seemed to imagine that I could withstand a lot more battering than I could, that it shouldn't hurt me as much as it did.

He didn't actually want me to get battered, physically or psychologically, but he didn't feel he was in control. This was the way I felt too. I had really believed that he was capable of killing me, though I knew he would suffer dreadful remorse if it happened. What I realised in the process of solving the problem was that I could actually control the situation. I could stop him losing control. I was no longer in danger.

Having understood how our interaction had led to our relative positions as bully and victim, I concentrated on creating practical change. This involved recognising signs of danger and learning to defuse potentially hazardous situations.

The key is to keep cool, as calm as possible. When the emotional temperature stays low, the situation is manageable. People build up to aggression, it doesn't come out of the blue. I learnt to stop the build-up in most situations, usually by looking for a constructive approach to the problem we were confronting.

It isn't always possible to keep cool and constructive, particularly when the problem itself is an emotional one. When I felt Colin was getting overheated, or if I wasn't feeling strong enough to keep the situation under control, I dealt with the potential danger by leaving for a while, until we had both cooled down.

Colin didn't always co-operate. Even though he said he wanted to change the way we interacted, he would nevertheless try to stop me following the rules I'd worked out to protect myself. He'd shout after me as I walked away, tell me I wouldn't face up to things, sneer at me for being gutless and 'running away'.

I dealt with this by reminding myself – and him – that I simply would not tolerate aggressive behaviour or insults. I was willing to discuss whatever he wished, so long as we maintained a civilised discussion. I was not running away: I was walking out, as I had said I would if he started to shout.

I had learnt long before not to answer aggression with aggression. That can elicit the most violent attacks. I had to be firm without raising my voice, assertive not aggressive.* I knew that if I were to try to fight on his terms, I would lose – he is faster, stronger and more ruthless.

When he was being rational, he acknowledged both that this approach to dealing with the problem was reasonable, and that abuse is indeed unjustifiable. However, we were trying to change emotional, non-irrational behaviour, and reason has limited effectiveness in this situation. Fortunately, we both value reason highly, and therefore have an incentive to act on decisions to which we have both agreed. At the same time, we

* See Anne Dickson, *A Woman in Your Own Right* (Quartet Books), for a very clear discussion of the distinction between assertive and aggressive behaviour.

did try to address the emotional tensions that were bursting out in this way.

I knew that Colin's violence was a symptom of frustration. I recalled a film that I had watched as a psychology student, of monkeys confronted by peanut dispensers that had ceased to work. They would try harder and harder to get peanuts out of the the machines, until they became so frustrated that they beat their fists against them. The parallels between the behaviour of those monkeys and Colin's behaviour were obvious.

But what was he trying to get from me?

One thing was adult human contact. Ironically, the more desperate he became for that, the harder he would make it for me to offer it. The more he wanted communication, the more I would feel forced to erect barriers to protect myself. To reduce the threat of violence, I had to reverse that pattern, if I could. But it is not always possible. For example, if he demands attention when I am too tired to give it, I just have to be honest with him; pretence doesn't work for either of us. I used to try to override my exhaustion so that I could meet his desire for attention, until I realised that this was one of the many ways in which I became a victim.

I had been putting his needs and desires before my own; this was another part of the unequal pattern of interaction that culminated in bullying and abuse. I had to understand that I was as important as him and that my feelings mattered as much as his – and should matter even more to me. I would no longer pander to his whims, do his bidding, or act like his servant.

By acting as equal adults, we were creating a positive synergy. When I stopped behaving like a victim, he stopped treating me as one. When I began to exert more control, he was less likely to lose it, so we both kept it together. Things could be rationally discussed and resolved.

Our whole relationship was changing; we would never go back to the way we were.

CHAPTER 5

HANGING OUT THE WASHING

The *Cosmo* article was, inevitably, a less cool and considered piece than I would write now. The years of abuse were not long behind me and the emotions were still pretty raw. But it did cover most of the issues that I had discovered to be important for preventing domestic violence, and it did describe how I had stopped the violence in our relationship. It also described some of my feelings and experiences.

'He held me by the hair to make sure he had my full attention as he shouted. It hurt. I told him it hurt. He didn't listen or didn't hear. I tried to pull his hands away. Failing, I thumped his hand with a torch I was holding. That was a bad mistake.

'He snatched the torch and started hitting me with it. I held up my hands to protect my face. Smash, smash. My hand took the full force of the blows. The torch broke. I ran away, bruised and crying.

'And yet I stayed with him. I don't intend to leave him. You've heard it before: I love him. I don't love the raging demon that sometimes breaks out when he feels trapped, frustrated, unappreciated: how can I? I love his astonishing intelligence; his wit, his physical presence, his understanding. He is a man of extremes; he has great depth and great power. Sometimes it's destructive but, more often, it's constructive. . .

'Fear of potential violence, of the demon within him, affected every aspect of our relationship. It turned me into a cringing, weeping shadow of myself. It stopped me raising issues that were important to our relationship. Essentially, fear kills love.

'As I came to understand the dynamics of the situation, I learned to cope better. . . Now that I know effective ways of preventing a bad mood from degenerating into violence, I do not live

*in fear. I can say anything I want to him without feeling that
he might lash out. So we communicate better, we're closer and
happier with each other – we've replaced the vicious cycle of fear
and violence with a virtuous one.'*

Then the magazine came out. FORGET IT, screamed the cover
in red capitals. 'Why I stay with a man who hits me.' I became
seriously worried. What was this? What were they saying here?
Why had they reversed the message of my piece? The whole
point of my article was that he *doesn't* hit me!

The contents page linked my piece with one by Tom
Crabtree, under a large heading, DOMESTIC VIOLENCE. I turned to
the article to find wonderful pictures of Colin and me, looking
very happy in the doorway of our stone barn; others with our
delightful plump sheep and boisterous dogs. But the distorted
message from the cover was repeated in the headline: 'Why I
stay with a man who hits me.'

I was outraged.

Worse was to follow. Unusually, the editors had tagged a
loaded invitation to their readers on the end of my article.
Under the heading 'How would you cope?' it said, 'This is a
personal account of how one woman dealt with living with a
violent man and is not a guide on how to handle this type of
relationship. Given the same set of circumstances would you
adopt Arabella's conciliatory measures to keep the relationship
alive or would you walk out?. . . Is it ever acceptable for a man
to strike a woman? We want to know how you would handle a
violent relationship.'

I began to realise that this article had moved so far away from
the conventional wisdom that my views were heresy. Tom
Crabtree's piece said that women should leave a man if he
hits her – there's no possibility of change, no way to salvage the
relationship. He offered no evidence, merely assertion. But his
was clearly regarded as the correct view.

Then the media reacted. *Woman's Hour* invited me to discuss
domestic violence with Jenny Murray. There, I discovered that
my views and the experience that informed them were utterly
rejected by the women's refuge movement. Sandra Horley,

Chief Executive of Refuge, was on the programme with me. She flatly contradicted what I had to say. When I explained that men could learn to stop being violent, she stated that men never changed; when I suggested that women had power in this situation – even if few seemed to be aware of it – she asserted that women had no responsibility whatever, except to leave such men.

After the interview, Sandra asked me how I had come to think the way I did. I told her about the insights I'd gained from role-playing in therapy, and how this allowed me to see both that my behaviour increased the risk of abuse, and that I could prevent it. She told me I should have got rid of my therapist. Why? Because she had led me to the wrong answer.

Clearly, Sandra Horley, and those who saw the issue in the same way, didn't want women to solve problems in their relationships and thus prevent violence. Not only would that mean they would have to change their picture of men as mindless brutes, but their picture of women as helpless feeble victims would have to be questioned as well.*

I began to feel that mine was not merely a minority view, but that *nobody* who knew anything about the subject agreed with me. I was not merely a heretic, but something even more despicable: a victim-blamer. How dare I suggest that women bring violence on themselves! Everybody knows that this view is the refuge of bullies, wife-beaters and other vermin. I was not only consorting with the enemy, I must have been brainwashed by him.

Another media reaction had more serious consequences for me personally. For some months I had been working with a woman who was to be the editor of a new mass-market magazine. I had won the job of agony aunt – a coup which would improve our precarious financial position – and had, for some weeks, been writing specimen pages for dummy editions. The

---

* Naomi Wolf's *Fire with Fire* (Chatto & Windus, 1993) discusses the issue of 'victim feminism', suggesting that this is a maladaptive development in the feminist movement. While she does not raise the issue of the victim role in relation to domestic violence, the problem she addresses is clearly linked with the one considered here.

title of the new magazine was still secret but I was looking forward to both the challenge and the comfortable salary.

Shortly after the *Cosmo* piece appeared, the phone rang. I was told that the publisher, and apparently everyone from the Managing Director down to the office staff, could in no circumstances accept me as an agony aunt. Not after *that* article.

I tried to explain that the point was I had *solved* the problem, that I did not live with a violent man nor did I suffer in our relationship, and indeed, that my experience of violence would help me to empathise with other women; but to no avail. I had lost the job. So I found myself with more time than I had anticipated to think about the storm my views had caused. Whatever reasons, experience or theories I offered, the view from every direction was overwhelming.

Men don't change, they all said. *You have to leave them. There is no other option. If you stay with a man after he hits you, you're a fool.*

There was just one anonymous voice giving a different view, one woman who shared my experience. I had written a piece on my by now familiar theme for the *Manchester Evening News*, which was published under the heading, DON'T GO AFTER THE FIRST THUMP. A letter arrived via the paper:

Thank you so much for the article, it could have been me talking – even the timescale. I love my husband and am so settled now but have often mused what was lacking in those violent times, with my not ending it. However, what I saw as my weakness was my strength – you have lifted almost a feeling of shame.

Thanks again for your honesty and guts.

Love, J.

When you feel that everyone has turned against you, one voice can be enough. One voice proves that you are not alone, even if you know you're up against a culture that believes what you are saying is completely wrong. This single voice encouraged me to continue to fight for what I knew to be the truth. Sadly, she'd felt unable to divulge her address so I have not been able to thank her personally.

Thank you, J., for your support. It gave me the strength to carry on, convinced that where there were two of us, there would – or could – be many more. Many more women who discover they can stop abuse without ending the relationship with the men they love.

CHAPTER 6

AFTERMATH

Two months after my article had appeared, *Cosmopolitan* published their readers' reactions. I looked over the two pages of letters written in response to my article with sadness. Sadness both at the dreadful experiences described by the writers, and at their total inability to understand my message.

Woman after woman described her experience of domestic violence, her feelings, and the conclusions she had drawn. All flatly denied the possibility that a woman could play any part in violent relationships except that of helpless victim. All agreed that the only answer was to leave such men – if you could.

Violent men don't get better. As long as women stay with abusive men, these men have no incentive to examine their behaviour and accept responsibility for their problem. Don't collude. Get out.

Violent men cannot be helped by a woman giving them her energy, her love, her stability and her body.

My boyfriend began hitting me when we had financial problems. My arms were covered in bruises and my body ached. . . Eventually, I packed my things and left. He followed me, cried, made me feel guilty and persuaded me that he'd change. I went back to him and had two days of bliss – then the violence started again. I know I'll have to leave him but, like so many women, I'm scared and lack the strength and courage.

It is not up to a violent man's partner to solve the problem; it is up to the man to grow up and face life's setbacks as an adult.

I was in a violent marriage for six years and felt worn out after reading about the ordeal Dr Arabella Melville is going through. I would much rather be on my own than have to work so hard at a man's problem. The final straw, though, was the fact that the ugly bastard had the audacity to smile out of the pages of your magazine.

for even suggesting it. The evidence that I offered – based not on unsubstantiated theory, but on first-hand experience – was simply ignored, the message rejected out of hand. It felt like having a precious gift thrown back into my face. But most of all, I was saddened by the total negativity of the magazine and its readers. They seemed determined to kill any possibility of hope.

Such a blind dogmatic reaction usually means there is something deeper going on than might initially be apparent. I believe that reactions like this tend to be linked with defending the status quo, however indefensible it might be. What I was proposing was change, which can be very threatening. I must have touched on something that is valued, something important to our current society – something more important than the unfortunate victims of male abuse. What that might be, I did not know.

What I did see clearly was that the present dogma ultimately acts against women's best interests. The letters reveal its failure: most women do not want to leave, or do not feel able to do so; those who stay are further hurt by the shame they feel at their inability to follow the prescription of the dogma. The dogma's OK; the women are the failures.

Do women need this? Does it not, literally, add insult to injury? The truth is that most women are not able to deal with violence, whether by leaving or by any other means. They don't cope, they suffer. This letter describes the misery and helplessness of women caught in this situation.

'Over five years with the same man, I sustained numerous black eyes, fat lips, horrendous bruises and even concussion. Apart from the obvious terror and pain sustained, what seemed equally bad was the shame. Not his shame, but mine because I stayed with him after each assault. . . Because I loved him, I would forgive him and he'd promise it would never happen again. But, of course, it did.'

'I have been kicked, punched, had fingers shoved into my ears or up my nose till they bled. My fingers have been torn apart. I've been thrown across a room, strangled and had keys

Violent men are always sorry. They cry, they say they
help themselves, and they say it won't happen again
experience, it always does.

I would certainly not adopt Arabella Melville's con
measures. I think she is raving mad. . . Victims of violenc
report their abusers, humiliate them and leave them.

What is she a doctor *of*? She seems pretty mindless and
me and her partner is ugly, mean, vicious, a bully and a

I feel like shaking her. . . she is absolving him of respon
his behaviour.

I had never seen anything like this before in the
These were the most distressing letters I'd ever read
and they were just a few from the massive postbag
received on the topic.

The vast majority of writers – 95 per cent, accord
introduction to the feature – were still with their abusi
Yet the universal belief was that the only thing they co
leave. It appeared that these women were trapped
helpless; they could neither leave nor change their sit

The readers' views reflected those express
Crabtree's article – but they were unable to follow
'The following should be every woman's stance on
he wrote. 'If, as my partner, you become violent, I ge
diately. When the punching starts, it's time to fin
different, something better.' A related point w
theme in the latter part of his article: 'No rea
woman; a real man treats a woman with respect.'

This sounds fine, but it does not help wom
relationships who do not want to leave. Simple
opinion do not constitute answers to a problem as
domestic violence. Women need something mo
those who are unwilling, or unable, to leave. It is
ful – and absurd – to tell such women that their p
'real men'.

Nobody was willing to consider the idea that
have any power over the situation. I was conde

rammed into my scalp by my partner. I've also been threatened with a knife. Our sex life is terrible. If I don't hold his penis correctly, he shouts, punches and throttles me. There is no foreplay or tenderness. I have often thought about leaving but lack the courage – better the Devil you know. . .'

The dogma does not help women like this. Nor has it solved the continuing problem of domestic violence. Women's refuges are full to bursting in every town. Some women seem to be on a horrific merry-go-round of violence: they leave one abusive partner, only to find that the next is just as bad.

The problem has not been solved because the very possibility of a real solution – a solution which gives women power to control the situation – is denied. It's all very well to say, piously, that men have to start being responsible, but how is that going to happen? Male social responsibility is no part of the laddish culture of the nineties.

Hindsight has convinced me that what I was trying to do was right. I was aiming to *empower women* by saying to those who really want to stay with their lovers that it may be possible to achieve a non-violent partnership. Of course, there are undoubtedly relationships which have no future; but there remain many women who currently suffer abuse at the hands of their partners, who do not wish to leave, and might in fact be able to realise their dream of non-violent relationships with the men they love.

I was one such woman. I discovered that it was possible to transform the relationship in a way that meant I no longer put up with even the threat, let alone the reality, of violence. My experience proved that women *do* have choices and men *can* change their ways. There is hope – if dogma can be replaced by truth.

One expert agreed with me – and, like me, believed not only that the majority view was wrong, but that it closed the route to understanding and dealing with the problem of violence. This was Dr Bob Johnson, a psychiatrist-philosopher who was, at that time, treating some of the most violent men in Britain: the prisoners in C Wing at Parkhurst on the Isle of Wight.

Bob Johnson had shown that these men, regarded as dangerous and untreatable psychopaths, were able to learn new forms of social behaviour. Through his work, the violence endemic to prisoners had stopped and the use of tranquillising drugs on C Wing had fallen dramatically. The transformation in the prisoners, as they discovered the roots of their violence and found more effective ways of interacting, was recorded on video. The evidence for Bob's assertion that such men can change is obvious to everyone who sees these tapes: it is totally convincing.

Bob was not able to complete his work at Parkhurst. Despite – or perhaps because of – his success, more and more restrictions were put on his activity. His clients, the prisoners, were dispersed to other prisons where he was not allowed to visit them. Eventually he resigned with a well-publicised open letter to the then Home Office minister, Michael Howard.

When he related his work to domestic violence, speaking to groups of women about how men could learn to stop being violent, he met the same reaction as I had. Nobody would consider his message, let alone accept it. It conflicts with the consensus that violent men, whether husbands or prisoners, never change their ways.

More recently, the view that individual behaviour in the context of relationships can be changed has gained ground. In some countries, notably the USA, the courts, tired of dealing with repetitive cases of violent relationships, have instituted programmes aimed at creating change. These require that both partners seek help in determining the problem and then behave in ways which will so change the interactions of those involved that the problems, if not completely solved, certainly cease to require the regular attendance of the police.

PART THREE

DIFFERENT VOICES

In this part of the book, a diverse group of women tell their stories. These accounts are based on tape-recorded interviews. Names, places, jobs and other critical identifying features have been altered to disguise them without altering their character.

I set out to find women with three things in common: first, they live with men who are, or have been, difficult in one or several ways; second, they choose to stay with these men; and third, they consider themselves to be not victims but survivors. In almost every other way, they differ. While most are married, some are not; some have children and others do not; and their ages range from under thirty to over fifty. Their education varies from the legal minimum to higher degree level. They come from a wide variety of social and economic backgrounds; some are poor, others relatively rich.

Although this is a fairly varied sample of women, it should not be taken as *representative* of any population. The majority responded to appeals I made through the media and networks of which I am part. They are self-selected in that they are all women who heard about the book and decided to contribute. To my regret, none came from Asian or Afro-Caribbean cultures.

The stories fall into four groups: women's experience of living with men who are (or have been) aggressive; unfaithful men; addicts; and men who have psychological problems.

Surviving aggression: Vicky, Louise and Stella are three very different women whose approaches to the problem reflect divergent attitudes, personalities and backgrounds.

Other women: Tessa and Amanda talk about living with unfaithful husbands; Marian recounts her experience as 'the other woman' in a long relationship with a man who eventually divorced his former wife.

Addiction: Chrissie speaks of life and love with heroin addicts.

Psychological problems: Sophie is married to a man who has problems with sex.

CHAPTER 7

SURVIVING AGGRESSION

VICKY

Vicky lives on the edge of a large council estate in a sprawling east coast city, a place notorious for unemployment, drug abuse and petty crime. Vicky's house, like Vicky herself, is neat and pretty. She is a local girl who did not have the benefit of an extended education or privileged background.

She wrote to me after reading a newspaper appeal for contributors to this book.

I have been married for eleven years, to what I sometimes think of as being the most difficult man to live with, alive today. You could say we've had a lot of problems, he was violent towards me and very abusive for the first nine years of our marriage, he was awkward and selfish and didn't seem to see me as a person. He did love me, he just couldn't handle it, obviously that was no consolation to me at the time. . . His bad attitude [was put] down to the fact that his father abused his mother and himself both physically and mentally. Now we are picking up the pieces slowly but surely. I have wanted to get out of it a lot of times but we do love each other and there's the children to think of too. He no longer hits me, he can love me now. But he's still frightened to give me 100 per cent in case I throw it back in his face.

People used to say to me, 'Leave him, he'll never change,' but he has, I just hope that eventually he'll be worth the wait. I've realised now that if I can help him change, if I stick up for myself, he seems to respect me more. . . . Anyway I could go on about him all day but I won't. I hope your book is a success, I now know that it isn't only my husband who's a pain in the neck.

The reason I wanted to speak to you was because I felt really alone. I hate to think there's somebody out there going through the same thing that I did. I had my family, but I didn't feel I could go to them. Everybody said to me, everyone I spoke to, oh, get rid of him, divorce him straight away; but the thing is, a lot of the time it's not easy to do that. Sometimes it's harder to walk away, specially when you've got a low self-esteem, which I did have.

Also, he's my children's father, and you have to think about them. I was just twenty-two and I had my daughter, who was under two, and I'd just had my son. My husband actually ended up having a nervous breakdown, he went into Rose Hill [the local psychiatric hospital]. It's been very difficult living with him, but you'd have to be a very hard person to walk away from someone who really needs your help at that time.

I know what I've always done is, I haven't thought about myself. When he was like he used to be, I only used to think about how he felt, and I used to ignore my own feelings. That was part of the problem. But now, I think of him, but I also think of myself and the children. I always think, if I'm happy, then I can be a good mum to the children, which makes them happy.

Paradoxically, as Vicky discovered, the unselfish behaviour which women learn is morally desirable – and which tends to come naturally to women – can lead to problems in their relationships with men. Yet she sees the need for changes in her relationship in unselfish terms – she is doing it primarily for the children, and having the children gave her the strength to do it. The desire to protect them is paramount.

I know it's not easy and we do have our ups and downs, but we are getting there. Well, I think we're there. We're just on a normal path like other people, we have our bumps. But the difference now to what he was, to me, he's like two different people, he really is. Tomorrow, I'm going to the dentist to have a couple of teeth out. And he's taking me. Before, I'd have had to force him. He'd have grunted and put on a grumpy face, which would have made it a whole lot worse, because I don't want to go to the dentist anyway. But it's better now because I know he'll look after me when I come home. He's happy to take me and he's happier in himself as well.

So Matthew is much more caring than he used to be?

What he's said is, he always loved me, he just didn't know what to do with it. He didn't know how to treat me and show me, but what I've tried to explain is life's not like in the films. Love is to be there if I need him, and for me to be there if he needs me. When I was younger, he was worse because he felt he could get away with it, and I let him. Whereas I think now that the bairns are older, I'm stronger, because of them.

I don't want them to see him treat me that way because I don't want them to grow up behaving like that. I've got a boy and a girl. I don't want my son to grow up like that. Matthew got it from his dad. Even now, he honestly believes his wife's lower than him.

When you say, 'like that', can you tell me what you mean? Can you tell me a bit more about how he used to be?

Well, even now he won't talk. I could bang my head against the wall. He talks now more than he used to, but one time he wouldn't talk to me about anything, and I found that really infuriating. It's so frustrating when you don't know how they feel about things.

So problems would build up.

That's right. In the end, what the psychiatrist said to him was that he put up this wall between us. And I'm knocking, saying 'Let me in, let me in.' One day, the psychiatrist said, your wife will stop knocking and she'll walk away. I said to him, that's just how I feel; in the end you think, what's the point of trying all the time if he just sits there. He'd listen, but never answer me. He'd just sit there and not talk. Another thing he'd do – there's lots really – but if I displeased him, he'd treat me like a naughty child and say, 'Right, that's it, I'm going out for the night', and he'd maybe not speak to me for three or four days. I can't think of what I'd do to displease him, something really silly, maybe nag about the decorating, something like that.

It is better now. But it was almost like being a child and I was being punished. I used to say to him, why are you being mean to me? I've done nothing wrong. But I realise now I did it all badly, because I was playing up to him.

You were acting like a child.

That's right. When he came out of Rose Hill, I took on the role of mother and he was the child. Since then, we've had to work out how to be two adults. It's been quite hard getting the levels because I could never make any decisions in the home, I never had any money apart from the family allowance which I spent on the children on clothes and suchlike. If we went shopping, and he took me begrudgingly, he would pay. I didn't have any money. That was another hold on me, having no money. So then, if I displeased him, he'd say 'Right, that's it, you're not having shopping money this week', and he wouldn't take me shopping. He would, maybe the next day, but he'd make me suffer.

Recognising that the children are supremely important to Vicky, Matthew knew that this was where she was most vulnerable. So he made it difficult for her to get food for them.

How did you feed the children?

I'd just have to make do with what we had in. If I had any potatoes, we used to live on chips.

How old were you when you first met?

Unfortunately – I say that because I think it was a big mistake – I was fifteen. So I've been with him fifteen years, we've been married eleven.

You don't look thirty!

Don't I? I feel about fifty! [*laughing*] I've aged a lot in the last two years; I laugh and joke about it but it's been very hard. When he was horrible, I suppose I just accepted that was the way he was.

How long did this go on?

It went on from first meeting him, right up to him going into Rose Hill, which was two years ago. For thirteen years I put up with everything he threw at me.

He was like that when you first met him?

Yep. When we were courting, I think I was seeing him about a month, I was standing on a corner as you do when you're young, and he was with one of his friends, and two girls went by on a bus and they were waving. I said, 'You shouldn't be waving at them! You're my boyfriend!' And he got hold of me by my neck. He cried after, it was the first time I saw him cry; he said he thought I was going to leave him. After years of experience now I can look back and see, all these times, it's been fear of me leaving him. I didn't do it, but the more he did it, the less I thought of myself, and he would do something to me, whether it would be just leaving me. . . I remember he had a motorbike, we were arguing over something, and he drove me miles away into the country and left me there, told me to get off the bike and rode away. So after about ten minutes of standing there blubbering, thinking what am I going to do here, he came back, and I got on the bike and that was that: we just carried on as though nothing had happened. He wouldn't do it now, but if he did, I wouldn't get on his bike, I'd find some way of making my own way home.

See, this is the difference. I just let him get away with it every time.

You had very low self-esteem then.

Yes, I always have.

Do you want to tell me a little bit about your childhood, how you came to be the way you were at fifteen?

I couldn't get on with my mum at home; we just used to constantly argue and nothing I did would please her. My mum seemed to think I was sexually active a lot earlier than I ever was. I think she felt threatened by me in a way, being a girl.

My daughter's ten now, and I hope I'm not going to be like that with her. But I don't think I will. To be quite honest, I think I've got low self-esteem because my mum's got it as well. I can see it in her now.

Vicky focuses on low self-esteem as a primary cause of her problems with Matthew. Yet she has succeeded in solving those problems despite still having low self-esteem. Clearly, it is not necessary for women to become totally confident before they can begin to tackle the sort of abuse that Vicky experienced. As they succeed, their self-esteem is likely to increase.

My dad never treated her badly – absolutely not. He's very quiet, my dad, very easygoing, but she does quiz him about where he's going and what he's doing, even though he doesn't go out except to work. I look at her and think, oh heck, I used to be like that with Matthew, I honestly thought he was having affairs all over town. I was thinking, well he couldn't be satisfied with just me, he must want other people. I must have thought he was so wonderful, to be able to have all those girlfriends! I look at him now and think, what were you thinking of, you silly woman! He's not that good-looking. But honestly, I really did.

So he was afraid of you leaving him, and you were afraid of him leaving you!

That's right. We just could never get it right. He used to treat me badly so I used to think, he must have somebody else, he wouldn't treat me like this if he loved me; he treated me badly because I always used to quiz him on everything he did, who he was with, that kind of thing; so it was a vicious circle that we were running round in.

Was he actually violent?

He was if I accused him. That's when he used to get violent. That's what he'd seen in his own family. The difference was, his father wasn't faultless, there was some reason. Matthew used to say, I never give you any reason to think it. But it wasn't him, it was me, and it took me a long time to realise that. Matthew could sit here talking to you, saying how difficult I've been as a wife.

I know there's always two sides, but right now, I'm interested in the woman's story.

I think as women we need help. I always felt alone, I felt so ashamed of what was going on.

Why were you ashamed?

I always thought it was my fault. I got a job, and I used to talk with the other women, and they'd say they were so happy with their husbands. So I used to think, why is it always me, what would they think of me if they knew what went on in my house?

I wonder what really went on in their houses?

I know, I know. I suppose I had tunnel vision. I just didn't realise what the real world was like. Then when he went into Rose Hill, I had to look after myself and the children, and finally I found out I wasn't as useless as I thought I was. I did a really good job of looking after the three of us. He'd left all the bills, because as he was coming to this nervous breakdown, he didn't pay any bills.

What happened to precipitate that? Because it's never that sudden, is it?

The doctor asked how long I thought it had been building up, and I said years. Because he was treated badly at home and he had watched his mum being treated badly. It was like living with two different people. He's not schizophrenic, but he had a good side and a bad side, and when his good side came out he couldn't do enough for me. It was, 'I love you' and 'Don't leave me', but then his bad side came, it was like a monster.

In the end, he just wouldn't get out of bed. Wouldn't go to work. I rang the doctor and he said, 'Bring him.' So I said to him, 'Do this for me, just come with me and I'll take you to the doctor.' I expected him to get a sick note for a few weeks, because I knew something had to happen. Then the doctor called me in and said Matthew had had a nervous breakdown and he was going to send him to Rose Hill. I thought, that place is full of nut-cases! You can't send my husband there, he's not mad! But it's not what people think. Anyway, I walked back into the room and he'd turned into himself. He was just sat, he wasn't there any more. He couldn't speak to me when I spoke to him. The doctor said he maybe couldn't hear me. It was as though he'd flicked a switch and gone off.

And that happened when you took him to the doctor?

Yes. What I said was, tell the doctor how you feel. And I think he did, and apparently he started to cry and said he'd been planning to kill himself, which I didn't know. So the doctor sent him to Rose Hill. The hardest thing was getting in the car and facing the kids. And all I wanted to do was cry and cry but I had to put this brave face on, which was really difficult. So I came home and got all the bills out, and realised what a mess we were in.

He'd always paid the bills because I never had any money. I knew how much he earned, but the worse he got, the less he worked, and the less money we had. And I was forever ringing up and asking for extensions on bills. I used to hate it because they talk to you as if you're scum. Anyway, I sorted out what I could. Then a few days later, it all hit me and I sat and cried all day. Then I got back up and got on with it. When he came back four weeks later, I was quite proud of myself for doing such a good job.

Since then, it's been like a big long hill. When I was always at the bottom, I was quite happy to sit at the bottom feeling miserable. But now I walk up, and I think I'm about at the top, I am carrying on.

A few weeks ago, for the first time since he came out of Rose Hill, he got violent again – he just seemed to explode. So I thought, right, you can let this beat you, or you can try and sort it out. I didn't want to throw it all away, just like that. So I cooked tea for the bairns – I didn't want any. I didn't cook any for him. A while ago I would have, but not any more. I kept away from him for that night, then the next day, I said to him, 'I'm disappointed in you, first for what you did, and second, because you haven't had the decency to apologise or speak to me.' So he promised to talk after we'd put the bairns to bed.

This is a crucial point in the process of change and Vicky handled it extremely well. She did not reward Matthew in any way after the outbreak of violence: she withdrew from him. This reinforces the message that this sort of behaviour drives her away.

Then, after withdrawing for a period of sufficient length to make the message clear, she reopened communication with him so that progress should not be impeded. In effect, the episode was used to clarify what was acceptable and what was not acceptable, and what the potential penalty would be if Matthew persisted in behaving violently.

And he did talk. He said he was ever so sorry, it won't happen again. So I said, 'I can't condone what you've done, but at least you realise you've done wrong.' I believe he hadn't thought he was doing a bad thing. All those years. I once said to him, 'Go to your friends at work and say to them what you've done, and see what their reaction is. Because you might think you're Mr Macho, but you're just a coward.' I don't know whether he did say it, or whether they just brought it up when they were talking, because I know one of his other friends used to beat his wife up, they discussed it. I think he realised it was something to be ashamed of, because I never had black eyes or anything people could see. I always got it in the head. I think he was kidding himself on, not thinking about what he did. And what I was doing was just letting him carry on, as if saying, treat me how you want. Which he did. Because he would do something to me and I would be the one to go to him, and try to get round him, rather than the other way round.

Now I know I can't change his behaviour, but I can change *how I react* to his behaviour.

With this comment, Vicky shows how clearly she understands the situation. Her statement, 'I know I can't change his behaviour, but I can change how I react to his behaviour', is at the core of her strategy for solving the problems in the relationship.

And I can say this is not acceptable. You have no right to treat me like this. But the thing is, unless you really think like that, you can't say it. My friend used to say, put your foot down, but I didn't know how to do it. I didn't know what she meant by that. I wrote these down, after I got your letter. Because I've a friend who's going through the same thing. [*She picked up a piece of paper on which she had written the points she considered important in dealing with a violent husband.*]

Number one is, 'Value yourself'. Which is what I do, although I never used to. I'm as good as anyone else. In fact, I'm probably better than him because I've never hurt anybody. I used to think I was the lowest of the low, anybody could stand on my head, I didn't mind.

Second, don't make threats unless you mean them. I would say, 'That's it, I'm going', and he'd actually ring a taxi to take me away. He'd say, 'I've rung a taxi, piss off, I don't need you, eff off, I don't care', but the thing was, he knew I wouldn't go. Now he talks to me, he admits he was always frightened that I really would go. He used to get the suitcase out and throw things in it! I said, what were you thinking of? And he said it was because he was so frightened I would go, he was testing me all the time to see how much I loved him.

But you did love him!

I did. I do love him. In a way, I maybe don't love him as much now, but I love him in a better way. I think the love I had for him before wasn't good because it was almost obsessive, letting him get away with everything. I always used to say, 'If you ever got another woman, I'd leave you.' Then one day I thought, well, would you? You let him get away with murder as it is. So really I'm glad he didn't put me to the test because that would have knocked any self-esteem I did have for six. But luckily I didn't have to go through that one.

Anyway, I put 'Don't make threats unless you mean them', for instance I'll leave you if you don't change, because they know it's just an empty threat, so they carry on.

'Try to get them to talk.' Which isn't as easy as it sounds.

Well, you did try. Do you think it would have been possible to approach it differently, there would have been some way you could have got him to talk?

I think maybe I was trying to force him to talk. Now, I'll say, if you want to talk, I'm prepared to listen, and I'll talk to him if there's something I want to talk to him about. I suppose maybe I was putting too much pressure on him, saying right, talk to me now, tell me everything. I used to say, if I could get inside your head, I'd have a good look round, see what you're thinking. Now, I don't want to get inside his head. Everything used to be him, him, him all the time. I never thought how I really thought about things.

We were having another baby and it was ectopic, we lost the baby. My husband wanted me to have another baby straight away, and this was when I started seeing a bereavement counsellor. She'd say, what do you want? Don't tell me what he wants, what do you want? And I'd say, I don't really know, because I hadn't actually thought about what I wanted – it was forever what he wanted. My friends were his friends' wives. I lived in his world.

This sounds so familiar to me! I've been there!

Been there, bought the T-shirt! Oh dear!

I know what a struggle it can be to find out what you want when you're always putting other people first. For me, it was associated with depression. Were you depressed?

I was very depressed after I had the children. Post-natal depression. But a lot of it was lack of self-esteem. We'd go out and I'd sit in the car, because I thought he'd be ashamed of me. Now I think, silly woman! But that was honestly how I used to think. I'd think if I was walking with him, he'd say, no, she's not my wife, no, I don't know who she is. I thought that was how he thought of me. When I was pregnant I used to think, I bet you think I'm really ugly, don't you. And now I see my friends when they're pregnant, and I'll say, oh, you look lovely, you look absolutely gorgeous. And I mean it. Especially since I lost the baby. I always thought pregnant women were horrible, but I look at them now and they look absolutely brilliant. I had a distorted image of myself and a distorted image of how he felt about me.

And he wasn't able to reassure you? He didn't tell you you were gorgeous? At some level, he must have felt that.

I think in a way, he preferred it that way. Because if I'd felt good about myself, I might have gone off with somebody else.

Vicky is aware of the methods Matthew used to maintain his power over her. Her insight makes it very difficult for him to use these tricks effectively now.

A while after he'd come out of Rose Hill, he thought he'd try it on again. I'd done something – because I didn't let him get away with the things he used to do – and he said, 'Right, I'm going to the pub.' So I said, 'Piss off then. Go to the pub.' And he stared at me. I said, 'Go on, then!' And he seemed to take ages to go out. I honestly think he was asking himself why, I wonder why she wants me to go. Then when he came home, I said, 'You all right then?' And he said, 'Fine.' So I said, 'Did you have a good night, then?' And he said, 'No, I didn't, I missed you.' And he'd come home early. I think if I'd said, no, don't go, he'd have got a kick out of it.

Again, that puts him in a position of power, doesn't it?

That's right. Now I realise that if you allow them to have that position, they'll take advantage of it. Whereas if you say, go on then, off you go, it takes the buzz out of it. I used to say to him, you get a buzz out of upsetting me; and he'd say no. But I think he did. He thought, I'm a big macho man now, wife's at home crying for me. I've been so silly!

Oh, we all are! At least, I was.

But you can't change, can you? You can't make yourself be stronger.

You come to a point, finally, when you are ready: then you can change.

That's right. You can't force yourself. I used to say to myself, I can't live without him. If he'd left me, I would have broken up.

But you found that you could live without him.

Yes, I could, and I could live very well. I did a really good job. Especially considering it was in such dramatic circumstances. And it was only three weeks after I'd lost the baby.

Do you think losing the baby was one of the things that precipitated his breakdown?

Yes. The last straw. There was quite a lot; he'd always had a bad relationship with his dad; there was the struggle at work, the bills piling up, his car got broken into. He was so pleased when he found out we were having the baby.

I was quite far on. I knew I was pregnant, but we couldn't get a positive test because it was ectopic. So the morning I got the positive test, I waved it in his nose – look what I've got! Real fussy. He went to work, then in the afternoon I started getting a lot of pain, rang him and told him to come home. I was in agony. The doctor came. I was rushed into hospital and they gave me a scan in the morning and said there's no baby in your womb. I had keyhole surgery. It was awful. I was in the bed in hospital thinking, tonight we were going to celebrate. What on earth am I doing here?

People thought that because we'd only just found out, it was easy, but it wasn't, because I'd been waiting eight weeks for the pregnancy test. But I knew I was pregnant, I felt it. We had all these plans – names, nursery, school – we were going to have a treble christening. . . all these plans just went. Whether we'll have another baby, I don't know. It's quite scary. I don't think I could go through that one again. Nobody seemed to realise what it's like. When I would have been six months pregnant, I dreamed I was six months pregnant; and when it would have been born, I had dreams that I had a baby. Even now, I still have dreams, and I've got three children. And I wonder if it means I should have had three children, or that I will have three children.

Do you talk with him about that?

At the time, when it happened, we didn't talk at all. I used to think that he wasn't bothered. I said to him one time, You don't care, do you? And he said, no, *you* don't. He said, you couldn't wait to get to the doctor's, to get back on the pill. Because it had frightened me. But it was a lack of communication really, I didn't realise how upset he was.

So neither of you knew how upset the other was, but you both cared so much.

It's such a shame, all these years, we just twizzled round each other, we didn't get together to talk. We'd just been going round in circles.

It wouldn't happen now? If this happened now, you would talk to each other differently?

Yes, things would be very different now. I understand that he has feelings, although maybe they aren't the same as mine, and he understands that I have feelings. Years ago, when we disagreed about something – anything, family, life in general – I'd say we'll agree to disagree. But he'd say, oh no, no, you have to think how I do. You don't have opinions of your own. And that's what it was like. Now, he'll understand that there are things I want to do that he's not keen on – like today, he seemed a bit iffy about me talking to you, and I explained the reasons why, about wanting to help other people, because it's such a lonely life.

I think he'd probably prefer that I weren't here talking to you, but now he realises that even if he doesn't agree, I can do it. I think women have to support each other, we get treated quite badly if we allow it.

How I've changed, is I'll say, look, I'm doing this. Are you going to be awkward? Because I'll still do it, I'll find some other way of doing it. Whereas before, I'd have said, oh all right then, and I'd have rung and said I'm ever so sorry but I can't speak to you. And I think that is the thing, you have to stand up for yourself. What you think's right. Because he may not think what you're doing is right, but that doesn't mean to say it isn't right.

This reflects a crucial element of the transformation that Vicky has achieved in her own mind. She has learnt that her own feelings and beliefs are valid and should not be subordinated to anyone else's.

It's the same with Matthew: he went to a group for problems of his own – he sees a counsellor too – and I thought, oh, I don't fancy that, he'll be talking about me, they'll be saying things about me! But I said, look, you have to make the decision to go. I am a bit iffy about it, but it's up to you.

The thing is, people say, leave him, leave him, but what if you don't want to leave him? What I felt with Matthew, he'd be 75 per cent horrible and 25 per cent lovely. But when that lovely person came, it almost made it all worth it. It didn't make it fully worth it, but I thought, if I could just have this man all the time I'd be really, really happy. But also, what if you leave them and find another one who pretends to be a lovely man, and turns into the same?

When the children were both very young, I used to think, what if I leave him and meet somebody else and he turns out the same, but worse to the children? Matthew never used to harm the children. What if I'd met somebody else and they were resentful of someone else's children? So I thought it'd be better to sit this one out for a while.

For me, it was my stepson, Colin's eldest son, who brought this one up. He said, if you leave my dad – and he could understand very well why I should be tempted to leave his dad – you'll just find another who'd probably turn out just the same or worse. And I thought, he's right. Better to get this relationship sorted out.

Yes. What's happened now is, I've changed. If I'd left him, I'd have stayed the same type of person, so if I'd bumped into the same type of person, I'd probably have done it all the same, got into the same situation. But because I've stayed, I've had to be stronger, I've changed. It's not the woman's fault at all, but sometimes, if you're like that, men can sense you're like that and will take advantage. So maybe I would have been a magnet to all the horrible men out there.

*You don't know. I often wonder how far our own behaviour –
behaving like a victim – makes a man behave like that. I'm not
saying it's the woman's fault – it's not something we choose to be.
But you're always trying to do the right thing, to be really good. . .*

That's right. Being a good girl.

That's part of the problem.

Yes, it is, definitely. I don't think all men are like that; maybe I'd
have bumped into somebody who'd have been wonderful whatever I was like.

*Well, your mother picked somebody who wasn't like that – as mine
did. But you found a different sort of man from your father.*

Matthew had his problems and I had mine, and we were making
each other worse. Because I changed in those few weeks when
he was away, and realised I wasn't as daft as I thought I was, and
I wouldn't fall to bits every time he walked out the door. Then
when he came home, he maybe wanted to act just the same, but
found a different me, found somebody who wouldn't put up
with everything.

*I imagine those first few days after he came home would have been
crucial.*

They let him come home for the weekend. It was awful for me
because he'd say, 'Can I have a cup of tea? Can I have a bath
now?' And I'd say, this is your home, you don't have to ask. I
think, I'd put such a front up, he felt almost as if he didn't
belong here, and I felt almost that he didn't. It took us a long
time. Before his breakdown, he was ruling the roost – he'd say,
'You gonna make me a cup of tea?' And I'd get up and make it
– thirty times a day I'd make him a cup of tea because he was a
big tea drinker, not even making myself one. Now, he wouldn't
even say it, because if he did, I'd say, no, I won't make you a cup
of tea. Sometimes he'll say, 'Shall we have a cup of tea?' and I
might say I was just about to make one; the roles haven't
changed totally, where he does everything for me.

The trouble was, I couldn't see anything wrong in what I was
doing. I was just letting him get away with murder. When he first

came up, if I'd let him he'd have made that an excuse. He'd have said, I've just come out of Rose Hill, you've got to be really nice to me, do everything I want. But I wasn't prepared to let him do that. I wasn't willing to let him come back in and take over again.

So you'd thought this through before he came back?

I wanted him to come home, I desperately wanted him to come home because I did miss him. But I didn't want him to come home on those terms again. I'd realised I could manage on my own if I needed to. I said to him, I used to think that if you left, my life would be over, but now I realise I could do a good job, probably get on better without you than with you. I think he took that as a rejection at first. But he went to counselling. He sees her alone.

I used to see a psychiatrist with him. He was a wonderful man. He knows just how I feel, but he also knows how Matthew feels. And we'd all talk. Eventually, as it came towards the baby's birthday, what would have been the baby's birthday, I started slipping down that hill again and getting quite depressed.

Matthew's counsellor sent me to a counsellor. If I go and I'm being silly, she tells me I'm being silly. When I first went to her, it was Matthew this and Matthew that, and she'd say, I don't want to know about Matthew, I want to know about you. She said I don't make decisions for myself. So she told me to make a decision every day. Because I was terrible: I couldn't even decide whether to go to the shop – shall I, shan't I – in the end, I wouldn't go anywhere or do anything because I was so full of doubt. And I'd say to Matthew, shall I go to the shop? I wanted him to rule my life.

You weren't taking responsibility for your own life.

That's right. I was letting him choose everything for me. He'd broken me. What self-esteem I'd had, I'd lost. I wanted to be told where to go and when to go. I knew I was doing the wrong thing and occasionally I used to break out. One afternoon I went out on my bike to see a friend and he came home and went back to work. That evening he said, 'I've got a bone to pick with you. I came to see you this afternoon and you were out.' It was an effort to keep it up when he was against it. Whereas now it's not an effort, because this is the way I really am.

I used to say, I don't know me any more. There isn't a me any more. But there is. It's all there. I go to work now, I work with a load of women and it's brilliant. But if Matthew had had his way he'd have stopped me going. He made it really awkward for me. I would ask him to pick our little boy up from nursery school for me, because I had to get to work, and he would do it but he'd moan about it, complain he'd lost money. I'd say, look Matthew, it's only for four weeks till he starts school, and it's only one day a week, but he'd moan, moan, moan.

One day I thought I just wouldn't bother any more, and I said to the women I don't think I'll be coming any more. They wouldn't have it. They said, 'Don't you dare, you get here no matter what!' I've been there three and a half years now, and I know now I'd have been so silly if I'd have let him get away with that. I didn't let him. I put my foot down. And it's paid dividends. I'm still there, and I still love it, and to be able to speak to women is so important.

I agree totally with Vicky. Women need the support of a group. Women evolved in social groups in hunter-gatherer cultures, where they would co-operate to look after children and other dependants.

I'm not the boss now, it's just that if I want to do something, even if Matthew doesn't want me to do it, if I think it's the right thing I'll do it. Whereas before I'd have thought, he doesn't want me to do it, I won't bother then. They're my decisions.

Do you think this change would have been possible without the psychiatrist and the counsellors?

It would have been eventually. It would have come on slower. Because the children are older, that has made a difference. I don't want John to be a miniature of Matthew, Mr Macho, and I don't want Lucy to think this is the way that women are. She'll say, it's the women that stay at home and have the babies, and

I'll say, no, Lucy, that's not right. I don't particularly want her to be a little feminist but I want her to know she's got as many rights as anyone else. She's learning. She used to be really quiet, the teachers used to say she couldn't make decisions, she was always afraid of getting it wrong. It was beginning to rub off on my daughter. But I thought no, I'm not going to allow this to happen, absolutely no way. Now she's more confident. I say, look, if you get it wrong, Lucy, it doesn't matter, we all make mistakes.

That was another thing I used to do. I used to kick myself all over the place for things that I did wrong. Like if I spoke to somebody and I said the wrong thing – as you do, you know, if you're nervous – I'd come home and say to myself, you're so stupid, what did you say that for? I'd go on like it for days, really giving myself a good bashing. And my counsellor said, we all say silly things, we all make mistakes; you're only human, after all. I couldn't have done this with you then, because when you'd gone I'd be thinking, shouldn't have said that, I bet you made yourself look a right idiot – going on and on about myself. My counsellor said, 'You're really good at that, aren't you?' You see, now I recognise that I am. And I stop myself.

We have a relative who doesn't want to have much to do with us, and I keep thinking, I'll ring her up. When I do, she's a bit off with me on the phone, so what I'm wanting to do all the time is ring her up so she'll be off with me. So I'll feel bad about it. I am good at making myself feel bad. But now I recognise it, I say no, don't ring her up, wait for her to ring you.

Now I recognise my faults and accept them. You have to admit the good things about yourself too. I realise now I'm not as bad as I thought. I had this distorted image of myself, I thought I was lower than low. Matthew's bad side thrived on that. He used to say, 'You're fat and ugly', and I would think, I know I am, I know. When I was pregnant, I honestly thought I was ugly and I gave him the go-ahead to treat me like he did.

It's changed not so much because he's changed, more because I've changed. He won't be allowed to treat me like he did, so he doesn't try.

I was giving him the power to treat me like that. So really, we were bumping into each other all the time, for being horrible.

He's done awful things to me, he's spat on me, and hit me, and banged my head against the wall, thrown me out in the garden, pulled me out the car in front of people – the list goes on and on. But the trouble was, I'd still come in, I'd still make him his tea.

You'd try to placate him.

Yes. And all the time, I don't know how his mind worked, but he was maybe thinking, this is the way I'm supposed to act, she doesn't mind. She crawls round me all the time, still does all the things I want her to do. He probably always knew he was doing the wrong thing, but I confused him by letting him get away with it.

See what I wrote here. I put, 'Write things down on paper', because I find that helps. If there's something I want to talk about. . . I wanted him to come to the baby cemetery with me, but I thought I can sit and talk but it'll go in one ear and out the other. So I wrote down how important it was for me, that I wanted him to come with me, I wanted him to grieve with me, I needed him. And he sat and read it, and it sank in, and he came with me. I can't say it was nice. It was sad. But it was nice because it was the first time we'd ever grieved for that baby together. We didn't take any flowers, we just sat and looked. . . We were together, that was it. For me, that made a difference. If I'd said it to him, he could have ignored it, could have forgotten about it, decided he wasn't even going to think about it. But because I'd written it down, he realised how serious I was.

So if there's anything that's really serious, I write it down and then I discuss it with him later on.

I do the same thing.

Do you? That's good.

I've put, 'Don't try to do everything around him'. Because when he went out the door, I didn't know what to do. If he said, I'm going out, I'd sit and think, what can I do without him?

Because you didn't have your own life.

'Don't listen to what other people say all the time, you have to decide for yourself'. Somebody once said, I'll give your marriage two years, you won't last two years. And I thought, she don't think we'll last two years, so we probably won't. You know, I was busy listening to other people instead of listening to myself.

'Don't force yourself into a decision until you're ready to carry it out'. That's what I always did. I thought I should leave him, and tried to force myself into leaving him, but I didn't want to. I'm forever forcing myself into things I don't want. I could have left him but I'd have come back the next day, I didn't actually want to leave him.

'Don't be ashamed, it's not your fault'. I was always ashamed because I thought the state of my marriage made me a second-class citizen. I felt ashamed at work because I had marriage problems and their lives were wonderful. Even though they probably weren't.

'Have some life of your own'. Not just his life. I do have to make a conscious decision to do it. On Wednesday I'm joining a keep fit club, and I'm definitely going to do it, I've made that decision.

'Accept compliments'. If anybody said something nice to me I'd feel embarrassed. But last week at work, I told one of the other girls she looked really lovely and she said, oh, thank you! So I thought, well what would I have felt like if she'd said, Oh shut up! and walked away. I'd have been quite insulted. So now I realise how I must seem to other people when I say, 'Don't say that!' I suppose it's having faith in yourself. I am getting there, I'm getting a lot better.

It's always like that, three steps forward and two steps back. But the thing is, you're making progress all the time.

That's right, you're getting there. It's like there's this big mountain that I'm climbing. I say to Matthew, I'm climbing up this hill. And then he'll do something and I'll say, You've slipped me back down again, I've gone back down again. So then you have to make a decision, say am I going to just stay like this for the rest of my life, or keep going up that hill? I think, to be quite honest, you have to do this all your life, you're always struggling to get to the top of the hill. Because there'll always be something, or somebody, that makes you go back down again.

I think it gets easier, partly because when you've gone up a long way and look down you can say, look, I was right down there; and you know how far you've been and you know you can do it. And you know, even if you do slip down, you can get up again. If you could do it once you can do it again. You'll never slip as far down as you have been. It does get easier. And you learn techniques, ways to make sure you carry on in the direction that works.

I think also, what other people do sometimes isn't what you can do. My friend used to say, you have to put your foot down. But that was no use to me because I couldn't put my foot down. It didn't help me in any way at all because I couldn't do that. You can only do what you can do. I would go home and be real mad with myself, I'd think, well, you *should* put your foot down and you *should* tell him to do this, so I'd think everybody was better than me, I used to think I was so useless. The one thing I thought I was any good at was looking after the children and being a good mother. I am a good mum.

The thing was, these people who were trying to help were actually making it worse for me. My mother, the first inkling she ever got that something was wrong, she said, 'Come and live with us, come and live with us', but then I wouldn't tell her because she couldn't give me any help that would help, all she could say was come and stay with us for a few days. What good was that? Because you'd only go back, probably to a worse situation. They'd say, well if you stayed here a few nights, he'd be frightened you'd left him. But I felt at the time, he wouldn't be frightened I'd left him, he couldn't care less. Because he was always telling me he couldn't care less whether I left him or not. You know, I was always so frightened of doing the wrong thing. But the thing was, sometimes you do do the wrong thing, you have to live through it.

My counsellor said, do you think you could ever get back to the way you used to be? And I said no, it would take something very drastic to make me like that. Well in February, my grandmother died and I was with her when she died. She meant a lot to me, she really did. And if anything was to make me go back, it would have been that, because it really took a lot out of me. But if anything, it probably made me stronger. Because it made me realise the important things of life. When you watch somebody die you really really love, it makes all the silly things come into perspective. No, I don't think it'll ever get like that again.

I feel sorry for myself, the way I used to be. I'm not mad with myself any more, because I couldn't have been any different. That's the way I was.

The more you beat yourself down, and the more they beat you down, the less you think of yourself. And you're just going back and back and getting worse. Whereas now, I'll come home and I'll maybe have said something silly, which I sometimes do. And I'll think, you silly bugger! But then I won't think any more of it.

The other day, somebody came round. I made a complete wally of myself, I couldn't wait to shut the door. And I came in and thought, you silly bugger, why didn't you just act normally? Then I thought, well that's me, that's the way I am. It will get better. He maybe didn't think anything of it. But I was sat there thinking I was a complete ninny, because I couldn't wait to shut the door in his face. I used to analyse myself all the time and never give myself any room for movement. And with Matthew, too, I have to realise that sometimes he makes mistakes. As long as you learn from your mistakes, that's the way forward.

When Matthew had that relapse and got violent a few weeks ago, he actually learnt from it. He realised he'd done something really wrong. So I found it easier to forgive him because he did know he'd done wrong and he realised the extent of what he'd done. I think before, he wouldn't let himself realise. He wouldn't realise what he was actually doing to me. I'm five foot four, he's six foot. When I wrote him the letter that time, I said, 'Do you realise what it's like for me to stand looking up at you? With this big aggressive face you've got. Wondering what you're going to do to me. Whether you're going to grab me, push me, shove me, you know, even if it's only for a few seconds, it's very very frightening.' I don't honestly think he'd ever thought about it before. Matthew always used to say he didn't want me to be frightened of him, but he was making me frightened.

Men have to realise what they're doing, and the only way they realise is if you can get through to them.

Yes. You see, Matthew was always frightened of his dad. I used to say to him, what your dad did to you, you're doing to me. He said, you'll never understand what he did to me. I'll never make you feel the way he made me feel. And it's only beginning to dawn on him, he does make me feel probably just how he felt.

Last time, a few weeks ago, when he had an outburst. . . it was a bit later, when we were sat at the table, the bairns were eating their tea. John had a plastic gun and shot it under the table. And I absolutely jumped out my skin and burst into tears. I was on edge. The next day, when I wrote the letter to Matthew, I said that. I said I jumped out my skin because every part of my body was ready for another attack. I don't think he'd ever realised it affected me to such an extent. Matthew would maybe come home and bring me some flowers and think because he'd brought me those flowers, everything was fine. And I would maybe pretend everything was fine but I'd still go upstairs of a night and sit and cry. And he'd get into bed and I'd turn away because he was a stranger and I didn't want him to touch me. Even his toe or his knee or anything. It was as if a stranger had got into the bed. He didn't realise that.

The worst thing then is if he wants sex.

Yes. Because they think it's making up. But the last thing you want is to let them anywhere near you at all.

Because you don't feel you can trust them.

With Matthew, I always let him, which made me feel even worse. Whereas now, I don't think he would even try because I'd say, no way. Not while I feel like this about you. He accepts now that I can be annoyed with him, I can not want him to touch me.

You wouldn't have dared reject him then.

No, I wouldn't. I think if I had done, he'd have thought, what the hell's going on here? She said no! We had an argument when he came out of Rose Hill, because I wasn't interested, and it was as if I'd done terrible things to him! He was absolutely amazed because I'd said no. I suppose I was rewriting my mind and rewriting him as well. He was having to get used to my behaviour, because my behaviour had changed towards him.

I say now to my friend, you can't change the way he behaves, but you can change the way you behave. If they're going to get away with it, they do. If they're feeling low, they'll think, I'll get a bit of power here, throw my weight about a bit, and feel a bit better. And while you let them do it, I honestly think that most men probably will. If they're like that in the first place.

Do you think Matthew's self-esteem is higher now?

Probably yes. But if you'd looked at him a few years ago, you'd probably have thought he had high self-esteem. I used to say to him, you fancy yourself, you think you're God's gift, don't you? But it turns out, now he's actually spoken to me, it was the complete opposite.

It was all on the surface.

That's right. It was all just a show. Whereas now, he probably is better. He's not brilliant, but he's probably a lot better, because he feels, what you see is what you get; and if you don't like me, that's fine. He does sometimes ask for reassurance; he'll say, all the people I talk to out there talk to me, and I think he's saying, 'I am nice, you know, people talk to me.' But he doesn't have to tell me that, I already know. So we're both getting better but we've both got a long way to go. But we've been through the worst, definitely. I don't think it could ever get any worse than it used to be!

I think as you get older you think, where am I going to go? For me, the most important thing was the children, I didn't want them to be brought up in that sort of situation. I blame the way my husband was on the way he was brought up. His mum and dad have never changed. She said, quite recently, that Matthew's grandad was like it with Matthew's dad, and Matthew's dad was like it with Matthew, and Matthew will be like it with John. And Matthew said, no way. This is where it stops. I will not be like that with my son. But the thing is, even if he wanted to, he couldn't be, because I wouldn't allow it.

You would leave. That would be the thing that would make you leave.

Yes. My counsellor said, he could abuse you, but he couldn't abuse the children. I said yes, the minute he started anything like that, I would go. Because I wasn't going to let history repeat itself, because it'll go on and on for ever. With John we do things differently. We don't smack them. I've made a decision now, and I've told Matthew, that we don't hit them and we don't threaten to hit them. Because I can't say to John, don't hit your sister or I'll hit you, it doesn't make sense.

Vicky is determined that the next generation will be less violent than its predecessors. She has not only broken free of the violence in her own life, but broken the cycle for the future.

She made many important observations in the course of this interview, but I believe that the most important of all was this:

'It's changed not so much because he's changed, more because I've changed.'

The reason I see this as crucial is because it puts the power for change firmly into the woman's hands. And the woman doesn't need to be privileged, or an intellectual, or to have material advantages. She doesn't even need great confidence. Vicky had none of these things. What she had was determination. She realised that she had to change her relationship and she set about doing so with courage and with love. She had help from professionals, but when it came down to it, she was the one who transformed the situation.

Here is Vicky's list in full:

Value yourself.
Don't make threats unless you mean them.
Try to get him to talk.
Write things down on paper.
Don't try to do everything around him.
Don't force yourself into a decision until you're ready to
    carry it out.
Don't be ashamed, it's not your fault.
Have some life of your own.
Accept compliments.

Nearly two years after I recorded this interview, I rang Vicky to tell her I was about to send the book to the publisher. Her voice had become stronger; she had clearly gained considerable confidence. She told me she was very happy with her husband, their relationship had continued to get better and better. He had definitely proved worth waiting for.

LOUISE

I knew nothing about Louise's difficult man – beyond the fact that she was eager to record an interview with me – until I met her. She had divulged no details on the telephone. But I knew the exclusive and charming village where she lived and I quickly realised that her background and position could scarcely be more different from Vicky's.

She arrived to meet me in an obviously expensive suit. Everything about her said – in an understated way – that she was not short of money. But her hair had an unkempt look and there were lines of strain on her face. She struck me as a woman who cared little for herself, for all that she felt it important to keep up appearances. She began her story quickly, without apparent emotion, and without pausing to learn any more about me than she had picked up from the newspaper article from which she'd heard about the book.

My daughter sent me to see you. We talk to each other about practically anything. The children all recognise that their father is a monster but we all love him. He really is incredibly difficult to live with. When she heard about your book, she said, 'I think you should talk to this woman.' Because despite everything, I did survive the marriage and I'm still surviving after twenty-five years.

I nearly chickened out on the morning of my wedding. I knew that it was impossible, that I was letting myself in for a very difficult time. The things that had gone on before we married gave plenty of indications of that.

I wonder how often women ignore warning signs that a man is going to be difficult, and go ahead and commit themselves anyway? This seems to be a common pattern.

Shall we start from the beginning? How old were you when you first met him? Had you had previous relationships?

I must have been about twenty-four, not a child. I was teaching in the heart of Leeds and it was very depressing, a very demoralised school. So I was going through a low patch when I met Adam. It was a very exciting relationship from the start; we re-enacted *Brief Encounters* on Doncaster station as a joke. . . we met when I was changing trains. It was very clever. I had to make a phone call, and as I stood in the phone booth I watched as a beautiful woman in a red sports car drove up to pick him up, and be sent away so that he could have coffee with me. What I didn't know was that she was his secretary. He never told me that at the time. But it put him into some sort of different class. . . He sent me flowers. . . He was very clever. He *is* very clever.

Anyway, we finally got engaged, and about three days later I had a telephone call from a woman who said, 'You do realise, I'm his wife.' And I hadn't known at all. He had completely fooled me. We'd known each other for six months and he just hadn't mentioned it.

This is a man who seeks to impress by acting a series of romantic roles. Truth and reality seem to be less important than fantasy. Louise is playing a part in his drama – and she finds it tremendously exciting.

He lived in Manchester, I lived in Leeds. I went off with him on several business trips all round the country. Nobody ever hinted that he was married. And when I discovered that, I freaked. In fact, I fled the country.

Were you in love with him?

Yes, I suppose I was. But not so much that I wanted to destroy any families. In fact, I was extremely angry then. I'd been offered a job abroad two years previously, which I'd turned down at the time; so then I took up the job and told him to sort his life out. He wrote to me in a desultory fashion over the next year; I wrote back. He moved to Essex and took up a completely new job and so I said, well, sow the wild oats that you obviously didn't sow earlier in your life. And he did.

Then my father died; if he hadn't died, I probably wouldn't have come back. Adam reappeared on the scene and we married the following year.

So he had sorted his life out, at least to the degree that he'd got divorced. He'd made that decision.

Yes. He had done that while I was away, and he lived the gay bachelor life for a while. But that year apart actually did quite a lot of damage to our relationship, because it made him very aggressive towards me in a way that he hadn't been before. He blamed me for a lot of things – his unhappiness during the time I'd been away. . .

Louise's assertion that the year apart *'actually did quite a lot of damage to our relationship'* seems extraordinary, in view of the state of the relationship when she left the country. In reality, Adam is using that year as a lever against her, to make her feel that she is to blame for the vengeance he takes. He is punishing her for making her own choice – and reasserting his control over the relationship. Twenty-five years later, she still accepts, at least partially, his distorted view of what happened.

He thought I'd been selfish, which was a strange way of looking at it. Whenever we had a row, that came up: that I'd deserted him in his hour of need. A very male way of looking at things, really.

Anyway, my mother didn't want me to marry him and my family weren't in favour, and I remember feeling terribly trapped because he was laying the whole destruction of his life on me. He'd say, 'You ruined everything. If I hadn't met you, everything would still be perfect', which was a bizarre thing to say under the circumstances.

I can see why you were doubtful about the marriage.

This was the clearest of warnings that Adam would blame Louise for any problems they might have in the marriage. Louise, unfortunately, appears to collude with him. Instead of pointing out the absurdity of the accusation, she *'feels terribly trapped'* – in other words, she falls right into the trap that he has prepared for her. After her escape abroad, he needs to hold on to her very firmly and he does so by putting this emotional burden on her. Had she been able to see the situation more clearly, she might have refused to accept it.

> I did have severe cold feet on the morning. Then I continued to live with my mother, and that was one of the happiest times of my marriage, when it was only a weekend marriage.

At this point, the marriage offered a combination of security and excitement. Louise was protected from Adam's potential excesses by the presence of her mother.

So what was it about him that was so attractive that it overcame your doubts?

> He was very dynamic, very amusing, very attractive to me... He isn't by any means so attractive now, he's gone downhill. Well, so have I.
>
> I suppose the other thing was that I had been used to being admired in relationships. I was used to people falling for me in a big way, and having to tell them to back off because I never felt the same way. And here was someone different... Looking back on it, I know it was because he was married, but I didn't recognise that at the time. He did a lot of things like saying 'I'll pick you up at six o'clock on Thursday', and then not turning up and not phoning and leaving me bewildered. The rules of the game were not at all like anything else I'd experienced before. I was nowhere near in control of it. That was new and exciting. I never knew what he'd do. He'd turn up at six o'clock on a Friday evening and say, 'We're off to Inverness, pack a bag, we've got half an hour.'

Adam sets about controlling Louise by keeping her constantly off balance. He knew what was going on; she didn't. She did not perceive this as a warning; it was one of the things that made him exciting. But the qualities that make a man seem sexy, stimulating and exciting during courtship can prove very difficult to live with in marriage.

Very dominant.

Yes, very dominant. Still is. Still is.

Sounds like that's part of the problem. But this is so often the case, that what's attractive about the man is actually. . .

. . . a step away from being something that you can't bear at all. Very much so. And it's probably the same for him. Because I'm very independent, and all the time he's been trying to pin me down, and he still is. But always I wriggle out from underneath in some way and find a way out that fulfils me. I've done it in lots of different ways.

I have never had any strategy for coping; I've never felt in control enough to know what my next step was. Things have just happened. Occasionally he's said to me, 'Why aren't you a better manipulator?' How can you say that to somebody? But he'd say, 'If you were a better manipulator, things would run smoothly and I wouldn't know.' That's so typically male as well, isn't it? It really is!

Louise appears to perceive maleness (and therefore, male sexual attractiveness) as involving dominance on many different levels. The behind-the-scenes manipulative role appears to be one that Adam characterises as feminine. He seems to be asking Louise to take control by these means but this is a part she is unable to play.

We then built our house and he went into business with some-one he'd been working with. At the same time, I got pregnant. I loved motherhood; I gave up work and wallowed in motherhood. I had two daughters and got involved in all the village woman things – playgroup, theatricals – it's that sort of village, a real living village.

But all this time I was having terrible trouble with Adam. He was violent with me. Looking back on it now – I never spotted it at the time – he was like a child, competing with everybody in my life to be the person standing in front of me. He would really elbow other people out of the way. He hated me talking to people at parties. At dinner parties he'd get suspicious if there was any banter between me and another man.

And then he'd thump you afterwards?

He'd thump me afterwards. Yes. I never really flirted with another man, it was all completely imaginary, but it was a way of forcing me to focus on him and nobody else.

Just as in their courtship, Adam creates an imaginary situation and has Louise play the role he prescribes within it. There is no consent, no discussion of the rules of this particular game; reality is not allowed to intrude. Louise nevertheless acts in a way that is sufficiently close to what Adam sees as her part for the charade to continue.

Just like a toddler, actually. You're talking to somebody and the toddler will pull at your shirt. If you carry on instead of dealing with it, toddlers won't leave you alone. That's how he would behave if I brushed him to one side. It's very peculiar, really. I still don't understand the need for it.

I've been there. He insists that you're not focusing enough on him, and eventually he thumps you, because you can't ignore him then.

Yes. Yes. One of the last times it was bad was five years ago. It was my daughter's eighteenth and we had all the family staying for the party, my mother and sister and his family and their kids – so we had over twenty people staying for lunch. And I ended up in hospital with this. [*She points to a scar on her face.*] I had stitches in my cheek, I lost a couple of teeth. . . we had to say I'd fallen. And that was because I was too busy looking after other people. Drink was part of it as well; drink disinhibited him.

I had a third child, Alex. He was a conscious decision on the part of the girls, Adam and I; and we all sat down together and discussed whether we wanted another baby. We all said yes, and we all regretted it.

I don't regret it now, he is wonderful, but he was a real trial as a child. I didn't know it at the time but he had all sorts of physical problems which manifested themselves in incredibly bad temper. He was completely unable to sleep and he screamed a great deal of the time. I used to go to the doctor's and he'd say, 'Well, you haven't got the patience you had when you had your first two', and I'd say 'I know there's something wrong!' But he wouldn't believe me.

I was exhausted. He was just impossible and he failed to thrive. Eventually I got to see a paediatrician who diagnosed a biochemical problem.

Anyway, that left a bit of a legacy.

At that time, all your energy was going into looking after this child. What happened then in your relationship?

Funnily enough, I think he backed off then, because he recognised that there was nothing anybody could do. It was so severe.

When Louise was so completely tied to the home, she was trapped more than ever before. Adam does not feel the threat that she might escape, and can afford to loosen his control.

Anyway, Alex came out of it and started to thrive. And then we realised – and this is part of it all, because it was one of the reasons I decided to stay even though sometimes I'd thought I'd be better off out of this – that one of our daughters was very gifted. She got a scholarship to a school for young musicians. Then it turned out that the others were very bright too, and they got scholarships too. But that locked us into expenditure for their education. And then I really did feel very trapped. Until then, I'd thought I could walk away from all this, but once they were into that, I felt I couldn't.

Did you feel constantly frightened? Did you live in fear?

Still am. Still am. We had a set-to last night and I said to him, 'I don't think you put the fear that I feel for you into the equation at all.' I don't think he recognises that a lot of the time, I'm battened down because I'm fearful about what's going to happen.

And he really doesn't know this?

No. He chooses not to believe it. Discounts it completely.

I suspect that Adam knows that he controls Louise with fear – but is more comfortable with this than with the perceived risk if she were free.

I don't want to put my experiences onto you, but my experience was that the physical pain was actually the smallest part. The worst was the fear, because it's with you so much of the time.

Yes, I agree with that completely. The fear is a precursor, too, because you know it's building and you know it's coming.

The possibility of avoiding action does exist at this point, during the period when warnings of impending violence appear, but Louise seems helpless in the face of the threat.

Some of the worst moments for me have been when it's been in public, and I've known that if I didn't get away quickly, he'd actually thump me in public. Once it was at a garden party in the village. I could see from the thunderous look on his face that something was building, and I was just desperately frightened. But I couldn't stay where I was because I knew it would happen in front of everybody. I barely got out the gate before it happened on that occasion.

It would appear that public humiliation is worse, in Louise's view, than any physical pain that Adam may inflict.

I've rung Samaritans, we've been to Relate – or marriage guidance, as it was then. . .

He went with you?

He went with me. . . I got him to see a psychiatrist on one occasion, who said he was a psychopath. Which I agree with: I think he is. None of which made any difference. But really I don't think it's treatable. In fact, I now know that. I have been studying the subject, it relates to my work.

Labelling Adam as a psychopath and asserting that his condition is not treatable absolves both of them from responsibility. It means that no action will be taken to try to prevent violence. It also implies that Louise plays no part whatever in eliciting the abuse – it is inherent in him.

She went on to tell me about her job, which she enjoys tremendously and in which she seems to be very successful. I cannot describe it precisely since that would identify Louise, but it is concerned with people who live in very unhappy circumstances.

All of this I did in the face of utter opposition from Adam. He said I was wasting my time, working with people nobody could respect: what did I think I was doing? I was being Joan of Arc. . . He tore it down all the time.

He was showing no respect for you, your priorities and your beliefs, then.

No. None at all.

How did you deal with that?

I just kept saying I needed it.

Louise will remain more firmly under Adam's control if she is kept from discovering a sense of her own worth. Undermining her belief in the value of her work is one way he tries to do this. But Louise is steadfast in holding on to her own moral values, which give meaning to her work. This gives her the strength to resist his influence in this context – with the result that his efforts to control her cease to be effective.

Finally, she is beginning to act as a survivor, taking control of her life despite Adam's opposition. Interestingly, he does not use the sanction of violence to prevent her from taking this job. While this could be because he recognises that violence in this context might drive her away, it is also likely that the situation is such that the probability of violence is reduced. There are two reasons for this: first, Louise is demonstrating her moral strength by standing up to Adam; and second, she discusses the issue of her job coolly, in a way that does not provoke an intense emotional reaction in her husband. Male violence is more likely to occur in an emotionally charged situation.

My job actually put all my problems very much in context. I'd get so focused on other people's problems, which were much worse than mine. Massive, by comparison. But my problems helped me to understand them. I could easily have battered Alex – could have killed Adam, too – at some points along the line, so I understood how people *in extremis* do foolish things, so there was quite a lot of empathy.

The job was part time for the first few years, when Alex was small, but I felt it kept me sane. Then three years ago, I was asked if I'd work full time as an executive. So I now earn £40,000, I have a flat in central London, and I have ostensibly escaped. It is up to me to come back at weekends; I don't need to but I do. Alex is at boarding school, he comes home at weekends.

So why do you come home?

Because I love my house and I suppose I feel responsible for Adam to some extent.

Responsible? [I am incredulous] How's that?

I've always had an overdeveloped sense of responsibility for other people. That's just one of those things. But you probably can guess that that's even more of a reason for him to try to get me to focus on him, because he's fading, as it were.

So is he becoming more difficult?

No, I wouldn't say that. I think he has mellowed a bit. He's become less. . . less demanding. He spends a lot more time with his friends. I wouldn't want to stay in London all the time anyway. I do feel my home is in the village. And I want to maintain the base for the children to come back to.

So the family life is really important to you, and the village, and the whole environment.

Very. Very much so. The girls say they come back to see him but they really don't know whether he cares.

Do you feel that's true for you as well?

Caring for me, you mean? Yes. He never shows me he cares. It's a very peculiar thing. All my marriage really, when I look back. He basks in my reflected glory, he'll boast about the things I've done, about the fact that I'm high-powered and respected in the city, but never to me, never tells me it's wonderful, what I've achieved, and aren't you clever, I'm so proud of you. I suppose I don't say those things to him either. But. . . he just never shows appreciation.

What about the violence?

That has mellowed a lot. The threat is still there. I am still fearful. It's probably three years since he really thumped me now. But he's come very close.

And you can't prevent it.

I can't find a way of stopping it happening, no.

I suspect that the violence may in fact have stopped, that it is no coincidence that Adam has not thumped Louise since she began to work full time in London. Returning to the marital home is now her positive choice; the balance between risk and benefit has changed significantly. At the same time, Adam has become less dependent on Louise, and is spending more time with friends.

The other thing I do know, looking back, is that when I've tried to be loving and affectionate and focus totally on him, it actually makes matters worse. Because he then starts pushing. He'll set me up to fail. He'll find another way. You don't love him enough so you've got to do this. And he keeps going till you eventually say, no I can't go any further. Then he turns round and says, I knew it was all a sham.

It's a very peculiar psychological trait but I've seen it in other people. He's determined to say, you've failed me. I reckon it comes from a flawed relationship with his mother. His father was away a lot and his mother made him into her little helper. He became the man of the house. It was clever in some ways – she gave him all this status – but it continued even when his father was back and his father's nose got put out of joint because Adam was top dog. They had a difficult relationship, him and his father.

Again, Louise is asserting her belief that the violence is inherent in Adam, that it is something that was fixed long ago and therefore is not amenable to change. Curiously, though, while she does not believe she can prevent it, she has recognised that she can make it worse.

But that drive and that dynamism was what made him into a very successful businessman. His business is worth many millions.

One of the problems with this sort of relationship is keeping a sense of your own self. How did you manage?

I've retained my sense of self-worth, but at great cost. My painting has always been important, I've always kept that going. But I did get very ground down. I got terribly depressed at times, feeling really belittled and horribly squashed. But every Thursday I'd get out of the house to my painting class, and I'd insist that he came home so I could do that.

When Louise stands up to Adam and asserts her right to control over some aspect of her life, he accepts this. But when she goes along with his demands and allows him to take control, he ceases to treat her with respect.

He was a workaholic as well. He took very little responsibility around the house, he would work till nine o'clock at night so I'd got the children out of the way. He'd then insist on a freshly cooked meal, which used to drive me to despair. He wouldn't eat a casserole or anything that had been prepared during the day, it had to be something I cooked. It was all a ploy, I know when I look back on it now. It was all part of the, you know, you've got to serve me.

And he would use violence as the sanction if you didn't serve him?

Not always, no. He was very clever at making me feel I'd failed. If I didn't do it, I'd failed. He still does that. Only last night he did.

You're still susceptible to that?

Very much so. Even though I know what's going on, I can't stop myself. Last night, he started with, why don't you come to golf? I said I didn't want to, golf is a game I hate.

Louise is again playing by the rules that Adam sets up – rules which are designed to ensure that he retains control and she fails. She seems unable to refuse to participate in these unpleasant games. Adam does not need to use violence at this point: he gets the same reaction without it because Louise associates her failure in Adam's game-plan with fear, originally engendered by violence. This is a conditioned emotional reaction; it is so firmly embedded in the situation that reinforcement is no longer necessary. It will not be possible for Louise to stop this reaction consciously: the only way is to get out of, or change, the situation with which it is associated.

Adam was well aware that Louise was not interested in golf. But she does not question why he suggests that she should participate, in the full knowledge that she would not wish to do so. Were she to raise that issue at this early stage, taking the initiative in the conversation, and perhaps questioning the pattern of their interaction, she might have been able to change the outcome. Instead of doing this, she reacts passively to the agenda he imposes. However, unless both partners are truly committed to achieving a more positive dynamic – and in Adam's case this seems improbable – it is likely that the one who has taken control in the past will actively try to reassert it. The price of freedom is eternal vigilance.

He said, why don't you walk round with us? you'd appreciate the aesthetics of it. I said I didn't want to. No, you should come, you should caddie for us. No, I don't want to. And it moved on. There were four different harangues last night. The final one was that he wasn't getting enough sex, and I was obviously dried up and tired and he'd have to find somebody else. And there are lots of them out there, you know, these women. I said, oh yes, fine, OK. They're all begging for it, apparently, on the streets of Cheltenham!

She laughed; it was infectious. We both fell about laughing at this ageing man's vision.

He has had an affair. Once – I don't remember it – but he said I said to him, well go on then. And he did. When I found out about it, he said, well you said I should, what's the problem? Christ almighty! I was absolutely livid, after all I'd put up with and gone through.

It should be nothing to do with what she had put up with and gone through. If fidelity was part of Adam's and Louise's marriage contract, then both should feel they could expect it. Louise seems to imagine that she has to prove she is particularly deserving: she does not see reasonable treatment – such as adherence to an established contract – as her right within the marriage. This sense that she has to *deserve* decent treatment, rather than expecting it as a right, makes Louise vulnerable to abuse.

So he stopped then?

Yes, he did.

So maybe it was important to him that you should put your foot down? He wanted you to prove you needed him.

Yes, he did. But sometimes I feel I am a failure, I've obviously made a mess of it, I should have been able to convince him. . . He's obviously got a self-worth problem, I should have been able to make it all right. You do with your children. You have to with men as well, to some extent.

Louise is expressing the sense of failure that seems to be very common – perhaps universal – among abused women. Unfortunately, the despair and self-doubt that this causes can block the ability to see the real nature of the situation and deal with it. She imagines she should have been strong enough to make him feel all right – when he was constantly breaking her down. Again, the underlying sense is that she does not deserve to be treated well.

Adam has only accepted what I do – my job – because he realised that if I didn't have that way out, stepping sideways, I would have gone completely. Because I had reached desperation when this all came. The fact that I could go down to London – and I've been going part time for ten years now – has been a great release, but even that was proving not to be enough and I was getting to the point where I really needed more freedom and I think he knew it. He's never murmured at all about the fact that I commute, leaving on a Sunday night, back again Thursday night, so I could go and paint. I always make sure I do that. Otherwise you lose these things. You end up watching television, vegetating.

When Louise insists that things should be the way she wants them to be, Adam accepts her judgement. Standing up to him is possible, and it can work – but Louise has to be totally convinced of her own views and feelings before she will risk confrontation with Adam.

You haven't been tempted to go off with anybody else?

I've certainly had opportunities but life was so complicated anyway, I decided that was a complication too far. I had what my daughter described as 'my cake people' – after I said once they could have their cake but they couldn't eat it. So I do have special friends, but there's no sex involved. That's worked quite well. Just good friends, really.

So part of you remains faithful to Adam whatever.

Yes.

Because of the parts of him you still really love or because of loyalty or your beliefs about marriage?

There is some sexual puritanism involved. Certainly, sex with him was better than it had ever been with anybody else.

Didn't that fade?

There were times when I felt I was being raped rather than being made love to.

Adam's dominant behaviour extends to the bedroom. At the beginning, Louise found this exciting.

Certainly times when I'd have said no if I'd had the choice, which comes to the same thing, doesn't it? And a lot of the time. . . it's difficult. . . a lot of the time, it wouldn't be mutual to begin with. Then I would get aroused. And so it worked out all right. But – it's not a satisfactory sexual relationship now. It isn't at all. Because I never really feel like making the first move.

There's nothing, in my experience, that destroys desire like the mixture of anger and fear.

That's absolutely true. Yes. I have stood over him with a marble lamp, thinking I'm gonna kill him! He was asleep. [*She laughs.*] I thought I wanted to. But I've never hit him back. Battening it all down is a kind of weapon, I suppose. I refuse to show my fear. I suppose in a way that's quite a potent weapon. You are kind of claiming the moral high ground.

You're telling him he can't really get to you.

He keeps on threatening to chuck me out. Says I'm obviously tired and washed up, he'll find someone younger.

We middle-aged women can be very susceptible to that.

It's true. We are. You don't turn heads when you walk into a room any more. Though my success has all come since I was forty.

My advice to anybody is: don't give in, don't give up something you enjoy for someone else's reasons. Because you never know where your life's going to lead.

Louise's final statement is the key to her ability to survive her relationship with Adam. She does actually understand, at least in part, how to deal with this type of difficult man, and she has succeeded in creating a life for herself that is highly satisfying in many respects. However, her relationship with Adam remains far from satisfactory: she is coping with it rather than managing it.

Ironically, at this point in her life, the threat of violence is probably more illusory than real. Adam's continued abuse is based on the fear that she learnt to feel in earlier stages of their relationship. If Louise could come to see herself and her position in relation to him more clearly, it is possible that she could lose this fear. But she would need to learn to recognise and understand the tricks he uses to remind her of her fear, and deal with them by bringing them out into the open.

Instead of using passive resistance, she needs to learn an active strategy of anticipating and deflecting Adam's aggression. She needs to be alert to his use of destructive games to control her, and question her own willingness to accept his agenda.

Adam has had little incentive to change his behaviour, but the fact that he did consult a counsellor and a psychiatrist at one stage suggests that he might be open to the possibility of looking at himself. Bob Johnson's work has shown that the most damaged and violent men can change. If Adam would consent to working towards a more mutually satisfying pattern of interaction with Louise, he might be able to learn a better way of handling the fear of loss and failure that appears to underlie his aggression.

STELLA

Stella is an athletic, energetic young woman. Smiling, she welcomed me into her sunny living room. Her fiancé, Tom, is busy decorating, passing back and forth through the room as we talk. Stella ignores him and he doesn't intrude: he appears totally unconcerned about the interview. Arrangements are under way for their marriage in a few weeks' time.

Stella recounts the background to their relationship in a very clear, matter-of-fact way.

We've known each other seven and a half years, been living together seven years, with a year's break for college. That wasn't a break in the relationship, it was a break in the living arrangements. I was twenty-two and he was twenty-nine when we began to live together. I lived with another man before him, for three years in total.

I'm not sure, actually, thinking about it, that I would describe him as a difficult man. I probably would have, a few years ago. I think, then, that I enjoyed being the younger girl who had an older, strong male with whom she wrestled; and I took a sort of – not quite a victim role – but I liked seeing myself as the weaker partner who overcame a big difficulty. So in a way I painted him as an obstacle.

So you wanted him to be difficult?

Yes. I don't need him to be difficult any more, I don't want him to be difficult any more, but in the beginning, definitely. I think this pattern has always been there in every relationship I've had – brothers, mother, father, everybody. I have this relationship where I like to imagine that I'm calm, reasonable, and I will play a supporting role, I will find out whatever it is about them that needs to be worked around, and effectively give myself a pat on the back when I do it.

It's very manipulative, very feminine. You always find an answer, don't you? I think maybe it's a – actually I don't know that having to find a solution is gender specific, but I think that being the weaker partner is a female thing, definitely. I think women don't like men who are weaker. When I lived with the previous man, the reason it didn't work out was because we both wanted to be the one that supported the other, so we were both being too helpful too much of the time, and left wondering were we needed, where did we fit in? Where was our role? And because I have this rapidly fading fantasy about myself that I'm very strong and very tolerant and very kind and compassionate, I very much enjoyed having someone who appeared to be none of those things.

He wasn't tolerant, or. . .

He was, totally. But I didn't give him a chance to show those sides of himself. We had a thing when we'd been living together for about six months, when I accused him of not being affectionate. This completely threw him, he fell apart and said he'd been dying to be affectionate, but I hadn't given him a chance to be, or hadn't shown any sign that that was acceptable; and he'd felt there was a barrier, and he found it very hard to give me anything.

That would create tensions.

Yes. If you've ascribed a role for yourself that the other person is reacting to, if I'm the giver and I've made him the taker, I didn't give him a chance to do anything else, so it did create tension, it created a total lack of communication. So we weren't talking; we didn't understand why we weren't. We knew we loved each other, we knew that pretty much from day one, it was always very strong between us, there was a very strong commitment. I don't know why, but we knew, or had decided that this was it. So then to find that it was falling apart a bit, it was very tense.

What was the nature of the falling apart?

I mean massive rows, things getting broken, doors being smashed. Having Tom shout an inch from my face.

He was doing all the smashing?

Yes. I smashed something once, and found it completely unsatisfying. And it was expensive, because the one episode, [*laughing*] it happened to be a plate glass door!

So I had a go, but it wasn't for me. So he does all the smashing, all the wrecking, Tom does all the bad boy things, I just stand there being a good girl.

The role that you'd put yourself in in the first place.

Or – I weep hysterically and go into a complete shock state. Which is probably what I need to do more of anyway, rather than always be strong. It might be that the only time I let myself have a good old weep is when I create a situation where in a way it won't be noticed. I have to. . . to say that I now cope with a difficult man is true, but the recognition of the way that I cope is to have a good look at why I chose a difficult man, why I perpetuate him being a difficult man, how I fit into that pattern.

Stella recognises that she plays a crucial role in creating the type of relationship she has.

Because a relationship is joint, and one of you is not good and the other not bad, but it may serve your purposes to make it look that way.

It can look that way to outsiders. Somebody else, seeing the smashed-up house, might think he's violent.

Once I had a bruise because Tom threw something and hit me. But my father threw things and hit me, so I think my attitude to that is quite lenient.

Curiously, Stella's experience of her father's aggression has not left her afraid of male violence. Later discussion suggests that the context in which aggression occurs is crucial. Although her relationship with her father was sometimes stormy, she trusts him totally: there is no fear.

If he hit me, I would just think, what a twat, I wouldn't be interested. But he smashes things, which makes me curious. He's obviously not setting out to hurt me.

It doesn't frighten me. I don't think it ever frightened me. I think, to be honest, it always had a very prurient vicarious factor. I don't do that kind of thing. I can't imagine letting myself go to that extent. It's fascinating to watch someone pacing around, ripping the shirt off their back. At times it's distressing. I've wrestled him to the ground and held him down, put all my weight on top of him, because I've been scared he might have a heart attack. But I'm not scared I'm the object of the attack. And if I have been hit, which has probably happened a couple of times, it's because I threw myself into the ring.

So he's not violent towards you.

No. He'll chase me round the house and shout at me, and stand about an inch from my face and shout at me, but he wouldn't actually hit me.

So what's that about, the standing an inch from your face and shouting?

He wants my attention, and that's fair enough, because I want his all the time, and we know that about each other. What sets it off is normally, we've been discussing something, and Tom has said, 'Leave it alone, I don't want to talk about it now.' And I want to talk about it now, but he's said he doesn't want to. I'm saying to him, 'You don't tell me when we discuss things, or what we discuss', and then suddenly, he's off. But we're always going to have those rows. There's no way round it. Because I'm not going to be told when to talk about things and when not to. And I'm not now going to run my life always being attuned to somebody else's needs; I have my own.

Stella's attitude ensures that she will never accept an unequal relationship which would make her vulnerable to abuse.

We had a row recently, and I just thought, get on with it, I don't care. When he smashes things, he always tidies up afterwards, he always replaces things. If he smashes things in the evening, you can't tell in the morning. We carry on as if nothing's happened.

Do you think you've become more tolerant of that than you were?

I think I've become less interested. I don't find it as exciting and passionate as I used to.

Does that mean it happens less often?

It does happen a lot less often, yes. I'm not encouraging it, I'm not getting what I once did out of it. I think I found it really amazing that I could have that effect on someone, that just by saying a few words, he could go absolutely apeshit. It's amazing to have that control, that power. And afterwards, he's always in tears, always very passionate and in love.

And that's what you wanted?

Yeah, if I got a bit bored, I pulled Tom's strings. But on the other hand, there are times when he will just be in a bad mood for days. That is a pain in the arse. That's a different kettle, though.

That's how he's difficult now.

Yes, the dramatic stuff is over. Now he'll just be bad tempered about things. If things don't quite go right, he'll pull things and break things. That is like a child in a tantrum, and that – I don't know if that's an attention thing, or whether it's just his nature. But before, I paid it attention; now I just ignore it. Anything about his behaviour I don't like, I just ignore.

Good psychology!

She is using the principle of refusing to reward behaviour that she wishes to discourage, even by paying attention to it. This means that such behaviour tends to become less common.

It's supposed to be, isn't it? If I ignore it for too long, that's when he comes and shouts in my face.

Yes. Because he's wanting attention and you're not giving it.

Um. And if I don't pay him attention then, it can lead up to a full-scale row. But if I know that he has started it, he's got himself into this state, I'll just find it amusing and I might go out for a walk. But I won't feel that I owe him anything, or that I was part of it, I don't worry about it. It's his business.

You seem to be very clear about this, and how you deal with it.

Areas of responsibility, I'm clear about.

Once again, Stella has homed in on a crucial issue in relationships.

Had you seriously considered leaving him, at earlier stages, because of this?

Yes. I definitely had. I definitely thought a different kind of man altogether would do me. A lighter-natured man, a man who didn't take life so seriously, who found little setbacks amusing. Then over the years I thought about that sort of man, and realised he'd bore me shitless. I like Tom. I like the fact that things annoy him. Tom is very real. Very human. He doesn't pretend to be anything he's not. He's got a lot of integrity, honesty, strength. On a good day – and there are far more good days than bad – he can be really charming, very funny, and most people who meet him think he's completely lovely.

The bad side of our relationship we tend to keep to ourselves so it doesn't impinge on other areas of our life. Though. . . the times I've thought about leaving Tom, as soon as I'm away from him for even a short space of time, all I can remember are the good things. I can't hold on to the bad for long enough.

So you always come back.

Always come back. Even when I thought about leaving him, I'd never ever think. . . If someone was to say to me, leave and never see him or speak to him again, I could never, ever do that, I couldn't imagine not having him in my life. Impossible. Life without him just doesn't exist.

Thinking about how all this evolved. . . could you tell me a bit about the sort of relationship your parents had? Were you repeating some patterns from their relationship?

It's difficult to say, because I don't remember them when they were together. I was about six when my dad left, and I have no recollection of a single day together with them. It's as though I don't have a memory below six. The only thing I can remember is a fight. It was some stupid thing about putting socks together into pairs, and it escalated into a massive fight. I think I vaguely remember the day my dad left. But I know they were supposed to have had a very violent relationship, a very loud relationship, and one thing I do know about myself is that if Tom shouts at me in the car, I cannot handle that. I'll have complete hysteria.

So that could be some sort of flashback to childhood.

Yeah. I don't think my dad was very good if there were three kids in the back fighting. I think he was probably pretty brutal. And so now, if Tom even raises his voice in the car, I'm a wreck. And he's always really good. He'll stop the car and apologise and open the door and get some air in. Because he knows there's something, some block. So yes, there is a pattern that's being repeated there, but it's ebbing out now.

I think the most important thing in the world is a relationship. It's the one thing I've always wanted, a deeply passionate relationship where each of you is the universe to the other. And that is what I've got. I think you're more likely to get that with a difficult man, because he is intense, he's probably more withdrawn from other people than a less difficult man. You're more likely to get the whole package than with a nice easygoing man who goes to the pub three times a week, who has a set routine. You're not going to get the heart and soul of him. A difficult man is more available to you.

A passionate man is a difficult man?

Yeah. If you break through the difficulties that have kept him isolated or whatever has made him difficult, this is what makes you pursue him in the first place.

Do the problems vary a lot with outside circumstances like job, family, money?

Yes. Tom's most difficult when he feels that I'm being pulled away from him, be that by family or outside commitments. To start with, he's a bit like what I call clingy. It's all very well for him to be passionate, but I'm strong-minded and I get caught up with other things really easily, so he'll start saying things like, 'I thought you were going to be with me, just me, on Friday night', and I'll say, 'Well, you know, we've got the rest of our lives, and this Friday I'm off with so-and-so'; and I'll be thinking, when I'm out, I'll probably make an arrangement for the Sunday, which I won't tell him about, won't invite him either; this was particularly when I was playing a lot of squash. And he was very good about it, really easygoing, and then occasionally, suddenly, he'd snap, and I'd say why? We'd have a row, things would get smashed and things would get said, like he'd tell me I'd ruined his life, and I'm a total bitch and complete cunt.

To start with I'd feel really hurt and now I think, it's not what he's saying: the thing is, I could ruin his life, he's trying to tell me exactly what a hold I have and if there's any risk of losing me, he can't handle that at all. But if he were to do to me what I do to him, I'd be a complete wreck, I'd be a little mouse of a person. Because it's normally me that disregards his feelings in this way, and I'm the one that goes off, it's him that's at home pulling his hair out and saying, you're really hurting me. But I say to him, why don't you tell me beforehand? I don't think he really realises that it's getting to him, he sits on it and sits on it, and carries on being easygoing and friendly.

So he's not really aware of how it's affecting him until he can't stand it any more.

Yes. And because he won't say 'I don't like you going out all the time without me' – he might say 'Why don't you spend Friday evening at home with me?' and I'll say 'Why?' and he'll say, 'Oh, you know, it would be nice', and I'll say 'Well I've made other plans that would be just as nice', and until he says, 'I really want to spend Friday with you, you're the most amazing person I've ever met, and if you spend Friday night with me I'll make it worth your while.' But when he says, 'It would be nice to see you' he doesn't take a strong enough stance, so I push him, he still doesn't do it, so I push him harder, he still doesn't do it, then suddenly he completely erupts. I do feel guilty when he's in that state and he's pacing, he's got one shoe on and one shoe off, he's literally snorting, and then I think I should not have done this.

He can't prove he loves me more than he does. I get tea and toast in bed every morning. Every single day of my life. He does all my washing. He does most of the cooking. If I say to him, this floor needs a bit of a hoover, he'll do it.

He sounds wonderful!

I begin to wonder if Tom might be the one who gets abused here.

He'll do everything. So when he has an explosion, I think it's me being immature, pushing him, and he's also immature. But then again, you have to be careful with that, because you're going back to the Joan of Arc, I'm responsible for everything stance. Because he doesn't need to erupt, and sometimes he doesn't, and he's given me a hug.

So how is it prevented?

I dunno. It depends on the situation. When we were living in London, Tom had a job so we had plenty of money. We had a flat that was fine to live in, and when the sun was shining I often didn't bother to go to work. Tom would ring me and say 'I hope you're having a nice day', really really relaxed; and then, when I pushed him, he'd laugh and put his arms round me and say, 'Don't spoil yourself, I'll take you out for a pint.' He didn't seem to get into a rage at all then.

Was that early on?

No, very much middle. We'd had a spell of being very poor before then, and I'd kept us going financially while he'd looked for work. We didn't row too much then – Well, actually, we had a massive row at one point then, it was building up in him that I was supporting him; and although he was doing everything that he could to get work, and doing all the cleaning and all the rest, it was building up. He doesn't like me to support him. Makes him feel guilty. When he had plenty of money, I didn't seem to be able to wind him up at all.

So I think he hates not to contribute, but it's a very specific type of contribution. It's financial. I think that's very much a masculine thing. Now I'm older, I'm beginning to understand a bit more, but I didn't understand when I was younger that money was important.

So it's not so much financial pressure, it's him not earning money.

He never cares what I earn or don't earn. There's never been a set pattern with me. I've always worked, never particularly earned much money, he's never put pressure on me to be an earner, any more than I have on him, but he has put pressure on himself to be an earner. And he's tried career changes and been broke most of the time we've been together, apart from this one period. He makes his own life difficult by the standards he sets. He doesn't mix enough with other people to know what standards they set, to know what is the norm.

But it is part of our cultural norm that men should earn loads of money. Status is so much dependent on money.

I would say there's a generation difference. It's not so important in my generation. If he talks to his parents, it's very important to them. But if he talks to me and my friends, it's not what we expect from a man and we don't expect it. If it happens in a relationship without love, it's despicable.

When you talk about your friends, are you talking about female friends, or men and women?

Men and women. At college it was a mixture. Probably I talk more to women but I'm talking to women who also have relationships that are central to their lives, that also don't run smoothly, any more than ours. But if you asked them, they'd probably say that we are most in love of all their friends. And I think it's because we're still so interested in each other. If we're in a pub, and one of us is having a conversation, and the other is about ten feet away, we always find we graduate to the outskirts of the group to hear what the other one's saying. If Tom looks as if he's holding forth, I always want to know what he's saying, what he's talking about. I still love it. Especially if he's laughing. He's got the most generous laugh, he just throws back his head. You don't see men laugh like that. He's so unselfconscious. It's sharing. It's not a laugh like he's scored a point. The best is if he laughs and no one else does! [*She laughs infectiously.*]

I always love him most then! I always think, good for you, mate! You think it's funny, sod everyone else! We often laugh, and no one else understands what we're laughing at.

Do you think he's changed during the course of your relationship?

Sometimes I think he has. I think he's come to terms with a lot of things that were obviously difficult for him. I mean, he comes from two parents who did well, got themselves educated at evening classes, worked in the same company for years, have a nice house, two children that both went to university, both have careers. Except that Tom didn't want the career and has spent a lot of time trying to get away from that. The difficulty is convincing him that it doesn't matter. To convince him that he doesn't owe anybody anything has been difficult. Although he acts as though he believes it and he'll do what he wants anyway, it's been very painful for him. The whole time, he's felt that he's bad, and he's doing something very wong. And that he's deeply selfish to be himself.

My background has been very much, Baby, do what you want. You've always got your dad to come back to. Doesn't matter how bad it is, your dad's always there. And my mum as well, but more my dad. Because my mother would think if bad things happen, I deserve it, whereas my dad would shrug his shoulders and go, well, that's the way of it, we go on from here. But Tom never had that. And in a way I think I've tried to be that for him, because I think everybody should have that. Everybody in the world should have someone who says, I'm neutral, you don't get judged here. So I've felt deeply for him that he's been so judged. Anyway, he's got that difficulty to start with, that to be himself he's got to be bad. Which is a hard thing. For Tom to be himself has been very difficult.

There are men, and then there's Tom. Others are mere mortals, he's a god. But he is difficult, there's no doubt about it. He is. But the difficulty is, how can somebody be so perfect, and yet be such a shit?

He doesn't sound like a shit to me! He's considerate and caring, looking after the house and you. . .

He's unpredictable. The difficult thing is the thing that attracts: the unpredictability.

Stella, like so many of the other women who have contributed to this book, points to close links between the problem with her man and features that she found particularly attractive.

He can literally leave the room in one mood and come back in another. It's very disconcerting. He can go out happy and come back with a big frown on his face. And I say, what's up? And it'll be something stupid, like he's spilt some milk. He can't just put things out of his mind.

It sounds as though the reactions are out of proportion.

Totally. When we were first together, I used to react on top. If he was reacting, then I was going to react, sort of get involved. Now I don't get involved. What I really hate is his swearing in the street. He doesn't mind saying 'Oh fucking hell' in front of old ladies and things like that. I think that's not on, personally.

When we were in London, he had a row with a man in a ticket office. It was appalling. I was really stressed out. We thought we'd have a nice day, go down to Brighton, just relieve some of the awful tension, when this happens with the ticket office man. All right, he wasn't all that helpful. But he wasn't unhelpful; he was what you expect from ticket office men. Tom has got his face up against the glass. He's threatening, basically, to beat the guy's head in. The guy gives him some verbal. Tom runs round to the side door and is kicking it in. Screaming and shouting. By this time the guy's frightened. I'm thinking, Tom's going to get arrested. Now, I'd think, go on, you bastard, get arrested, I'll see you at home in a couple of days. It's not that I don't love him, just that I don't want to play that game. Well at that time, I grabbed him out of the station, I'm pulling him along the road. Obviously I'm gonna get hurt, he's in that much of a frenzy. I'm pulling him, he's pushing me, I'm flying into things. At any point, though, I could have got the train to Brighton. He then kicks a bus shelter. I think he may have smashed it. By the time we get home, there's no way I can get out of that situation. I wouldn't say I was frightened, but when I tried to leave, he locked me in.

So he has done that. If we're in the middle of a row, I'm not allowed to leave. He will stop me getting out the door. We had a row recently, and I tried to get out, and he stood in front of the door. He'll push me and shake me and I'm not allowed to go.

That sounds scary.

Not when you look at the backlog of it, which is what led to the row. I've fully participated in that, then suddenly I decide I've had enough and I'm walking out. Why should I say I've had enough, I'm going? I think a lot of women do get hurt in rows, a lot are happy to be victims, and they must see, if they participate in the build-up, if they take part in the row, they can't suddenly say right, ding ding, time out.

Stella has raised an interesting point. If a woman does not want to deal with the consequences of an emotional storm, she should avoid participating in the build-up in the first place.

I'm not saying men have emotions you must protect them from, but I do think that if you're going to have a row, then you're involved. That's not to say when you walk in the door and some-body starts shouting at you, you should stay – yeah, then, turn around and walk out. And I can do that. There just comes a point when you cannot walk away from it. There's time before that to walk away, to say, oh Tom, come on, I don't need this, calm down; but if it's got to the point where we're really at each other's throats, I can't say I've had enough and I'm going for a walk. I accept that. Obviously he's not going to let me go. Why should he?

I know what it's like to be really really angry, and it's unbe-lievable. It is amazing. I don't normally get it, but it's an unbe-lievable feeling. It's completely consuming. It's ungovernable. All I want to do is hurt Tom when I feel like that. And I have done.

Is Stella telling the other side of the story here? This sounds like the apparently uncontrollable rage that victims of violence sometimes confront.

I've thumped him and kicked him and walloped him, and he hasn't reacted. I think because it stunned him, actually. It's like with somebody who's mentally ill, if you shout louder than them, you make a difference. About three times I've really gone spare, berserk, and I haven't thought, I've just wanted to hurt him. You just don't think, you feel. So I know if he's in that situation, I understand. I feel more compassionate.

It is a potentially dangerous situation, though, whichever way it happens.

Yeah. But if Tom feels that bad, he'll go into another room, shout don't come near me, don't come anywhere near me. But over the last seven years, that's happened less and less. In the beginning it didn't happen at all. Then there was a phase when it happened a hell of a lot. It was when I wasn't sure that he had done enough to win me. Six months we'd been living together. I was thinking, is this it, is this it, you come home every night and it's harmonious? I started to want more and I think Tom was just scared to death that it was a rebound and I was off. All my very close friends will say, they never know how long I'll stay anywhere. There's something about me that makes people think, she's not stable, she doesn't put down roots. I can't reassure them. Which astounds me, because I know that I really love people, but they don't feel it. Tom may well have felt that too.

But he doesn't feel that now.

No. Not now. Not any more. No, he's convinced. And I think marrying him, as well, is another conviction. He's pleased about that. When we thought of calling it off, he said he really would like to get married, it meant a lot to him. And I said it would mean a lot to me too, so we'll go and do it. I didn't realise he had this need to be reinforced in what is a huge investment to him.

Yes – his whole life.

Everything. Heart and soul. I've asked for it and he's given it. I've said to him, if I couldn't be someone's number one, top of the list, no choice, it's got to be me every time, then it isn't gonna work, because that's what I'm like, and that's what he offered. But it's warts and all, isn't it?

Stella and Tom had been married for a year and a half when I last spoke to her. She told me they were happier than they had ever been before, and still madly, passionately in love. Neither found the other at all difficult to live with.

CHAPTER 8

OTHER WOMEN

For two of the three women whose stories are told in this chapter, the problem is the man's infidelity. These are not casual affairs, but relationships that are acknowledged to be important to the men concerned. The third woman's situation is rather different. I was invited to talk to her as a woman who had remained faithful to a man who refused, for many years, to commit himself totally either to her or to his ex-wife; but her story had an unexpected twist.

TESSA

Tessa and Frank live in a beautiful house facing the sea. She has a busy acupuncture practice and he is an artist. They have converted one part of the house into a restaurant/gallery where Frank shows his work. Tessa and I meet to talk in her room; it is warm, comfortable and quiet.

> Frank and I have lived together for fifteen years. I'd had a five-year relationship with my first boyfriend; we didn't actually live together but we had a very steady relationship. Then I met somebody else and fell madly in love with him, so I thought, and got married after a few weeks. Completely and utterly crazy!
>
> He went off sex as soon as we got married, but I stayed with him for five years. He was quite a disturbed person, he was having psychiatric help when I met him and I think I thought I could rescue him; that was my kind of agenda. Towards the end, he installed somebody in the house we lived in and I went off and found somebody else because I was just totally pissed off with the whole thing.
>
> She was married. It was all completely chaotic. It was lucky we didn't have children, unbelievably lucky, because that would

have been catastrophic. I think he was a manic depressive, he was on medication when I met him, but I sort of rescued him and he got better. He treated me really badly, like dirt. But maybe because of my religious upbringing I felt I just had to stay with him and stick it out. Then when things got really bad I realised I didn't have to stay, so we split up.

I met Frank eight years later. I had a lot of relationships in between, so I was quite mature. I lived with somebody else for three years; that was quite nice in a way but he was terribly passive and whenever there was a question about what we should do, it was always 'whatever you want', and that used to drive me crazy. I don't like men like that. So we split up.

I had a period – a reaction against my marriage – I suppose what you might call a promiscuous phase – when I had lots and lots of partners. Which was quite fun in a way, quite wacky. But then I started thinking, at the beginning of my thirties, that I should settle down. I really wanted to have a child before it was too late. I'd had one of my ovaries removed when I was a teenager, so I was wondering if I was fertile or not. Anyway, I was in the middle of one of these rather wild and wacky relationships. It was quite liberating, because although he was totally unsuitable, we just had this amazing sexual relationship. I'd never felt like that. He was a real womaniser, a bad lot in lots of ways, just really good fun. We just used to leap into bed. Anyway, he went off with somebody else and I met Frank.

I was a social worker at the time and he was working at a day centre where I had a couple of clients. It was quite funny because I had a student who fancied Frank, and I remember her talking about him and saying how much she liked him. I hadn't really noticed him; I thought he was terribly intense, very into his head, as he still is. I remember thinking, when I first met him, what a pretentious creep!

Not exactly love at first sight!

No. He was so intellectual, it put me off. And then I happened to bump into him one day, some time later. And you know how you suddenly see somebody in a different light? I was terribly busy, racing round, and I just bumped into him. I said, oh, you must come round to supper one day, which in retrospect was quite daring! Though I suppose, given my past, I was into being quite daring with people. He said that would be great, and I rang him up a few days later and invited him round.

That was it, really. We got terribly drunk, which is not me at all, I drink very little. But I got totally overwhelmed by it all. And stoned. He brought some dope round. God, I was totally off my head!

Why did you get so overwhelmed? There was obviously something going on.

I don't know; intuition, probably. My first marriage had been such a disaster that I was afraid of thinking about committing myself. But I think I did have a strong sense that. . . not like, this is it, but some sense, some inner sense.

Anyhow, he moved into my flat, and we've been together ever since.

And you got married.

He gets quite cross about this, but we did actually marry because I was pregnant. We made a conscious decision; I said that I wanted a child and that was fine by him. But because both of us had had disastrous first marriages, we made a decision that we were going to be together for a year before I'd try to get pregnant.

So there still wasn't any certainty that this was going to be a lasting relationship.

No. In some ways I thought it was, but because I'd been wrong in the past, I wanted to be sure. I didn't want to have a child with somebody and then quickly split up. And then the moment the year was over, I stopped using contraception and got pregnant within a few weeks. It was incredible, I was lucky. Then when I was about four months pregnant, we got married.

We had a really nice wedding party, that was brilliant. Frank says that I agreed at the time that he was free to have other relationships; that's come up a lot recently.

You don't remember that?

I don't remember that at all, no. I've been having counselling recently and my counsellor says it's irrelevant. Contracts change all the time. The fact that I agreed to that fourteen years ago doesn't matter if I feel totally different now. And it does feel very different now. But Frank sees that as part of the agreement when we got married: that we were both free.

The world was different fourteen years ago, wasn't it? It felt less risky, having relationships with other people, and one's partner having relationships with other people.

Yes. The world was a different place then. Frank did have a couple of relationships early on. But I don't remember feeling threatened by them; they were both quite brief and on the side, as it were.

How did that work? Was he quite open about them?

It's funny, I don't have a good memory of that. I think one was just a one-night stand and the other was someone he just saw occasionally.

Having had a lot of relationships yourself, you knew that you could have sex with people and it didn't necessarily have a lot of significance.

Yes, that's right. I felt it was very much like that and I didn't pay much attention to it.

But you didn't have other partners.

I didn't. Which is odd, looking back. I'd had such a hectic time in my twenties and thirties, but I haven't had sex with anybody but Frank for fifteen years. I think I'd find it very difficult now. I do see myself as monogamous. I think it's to do with becoming a mother; having a child does change your relationship. I can't say how – I find it very difficult to put into words. But I'm sure it has. I think possibly, if I'd had a child with my first husband, my life would have been totally different. I wouldn't have had all those wild affairs. I can't explain it: it's just something that has happened, that I'm aware of within myself.

We've had incredible ups and downs, but I would say we've had a very good relationship, certainly comparing it with other people's. I think I've been lucky. Comparing it with Frank's first marriage, and my first marriage, it's totally different. We share a lot, we have a lot of the same opinions, we're interested in a lot of the same things. We have amazing differences as well: I do things he's not interested in, like swimming and acupuncture. He's not interested in swimming but I'm passionate about it – I'd swim every day, if I could. He's not into exercise. He just can't be bothered. But I love it.

We had a lovely house in London and we worked really hard on it. Diana was a baby and I had her in a sling while I did the decorating. It looked beautiful when we sold it, like a show house. We made an absolute fortune on it, and bought this, cash, and still had money over to build the gallery. I felt quite guilty about it! Mind you, we worked incredibly hard. We looked after Diana completely together. That was lovely.

We'd planned all along to move out of the city. We'd decided to buy a big house and set up the restaurant so Frank could sell his paintings.

That was totally knackering, having to cook all those meals, having to work when everybody else was on the beach. We made enough money, we were very lucky, but it also took an incredible toll on both of us. Frank found it exhausting, constantly having to be on call to people; and I had the feeling all the time that I didn't have any life. . . A gay friend said to me, you've just given up your life to Frank. She said it in quite a cruel way, actually; very cutting. And I really thought, then, gosh, I don't have a life of my own, I'm just the cook. And it really felt, I need to do something that's for me.

So I went on a healing course, but that wasn't enough either. I needed something that would stimulate me intellectually. Then I met a woman who did acupuncture and I was really interested in that. That was the point when I thought, right, I've got to do something, so that was when I started my training.

I think that was an important turning point in my life because that was when I started doing something I wanted to do, something I was really interested in.

How long have you been doing that now?

Six years. We'd been here about four or five years when I started that. I think it's helped me a lot. I opened up tremendously.
Looking back, I think Frank's been quite threatened by that,
actually. Because it's like he's seen me developing myself in a
completely different way. It really changed dramatically. I wanted some space, didn't want to do something that was tied up
with his work.

I think that was the point at which Frank decided that extra
marital relationships were more important to him.

You've told me you felt very threatened by his models.

Yes, that's always been an ongoing saga. More since we've been
here. When we were in London it was more peripheral, but it's an
extraordinary situation, really, when you think about it, somebody paying women, beautiful women, to take their clothes off.
It's just something I've always been very conscious of. I've read
quite a lot of biographies and autobiographies of artists; I know
that they often do fall in love with, and have sex with, their
models. I read Eric Gill's biography. . . oh God!. . . I think I get off
very lightly, compared with his wife. I mean his wife must have
been a positive martyr, a saint, because he was a quite extraordinary man. He was totally extreme.

*Artists are indeed notorious for this, and for being particularly
difficult to live with.*

It's something that I've always felt. Frank has had some extraordinary models. He had this woman called Nicola who would – I
mean – she – ah – she ripped – she –. Tessa is too choked with
emotion to finish her sentence but mimics a woman ripping her
clothes off in a most exuberant manner.

I'd be in the kitchen cooking, slaving away, thoroughly kind of
downtrodden and dowdy, and she – she was always looking at
herself in the mirror. She'd stretch luxuriantly and go, 'Oh God,
this is the life. This is the life,' she'd say. 'Lying doing nothing,
getting paid for it', and some comment – I can't remember –
about Frank. . . I just thought, you cow.

She was living in the house with us. She really got up my

nose. It takes quite a lot, actually, for things to get to me, but that did. I couldn't say anything about it, I couldn't do a thing, I just felt completely gagged. I thought, if I'm unpleasant it'll just create an unpleasant atmosphere in the house.

There was a real edge with Nicola. Frank's had a quite a few models here and one woman was really sweet. I got to know her quite well, and her partner. I remember one time I saw her in the kitchen when she was modelling for Frank, and she put her arms round me and gave me a big hug. And she said, 'Are you all right? I really worry about you.' I just thought that was so nice, for somebody actually to realise what it did to me sometimes. It touched my heart, that she understood what it must feel like to be stuck in the kitchen and Frank painting and, you know, getting off on all these beautiful, much younger women.

And also he was expressing himself, doing what he really wanted to do.

Yes, he was, exactly, and I wasn't. So I felt really trapped.

But you didn't go off and have affairs.

No. No! There were a few times when I thought of doing that, and I just felt freaked. I knew that if that happened, I'd just bugger off. I had a strong feeling that if I met somebody who actually triggered. . . I haven't said this to anybody, but I did feel quite badly treated sometimes. I felt that he put his needs first. I mean, I do quite often now. I feel he puts his needs way above mine. I have talked to him about that. I felt that if I'd met somebody who put my needs a bit more in the fore, that that would be it.

Isn't that a reflection of the difference between you and him? You are a very loving, giving person, much more than he is. There's a bit of an edge to him.

Yes. Of course, he can't see that. He finds it very hard to see that. One of the things that upsets me is that when very beautiful women come to the house – not necessarily his models, but more often than not – he has a totally different way of relating to them. It's like, he's very kind of seductive. Not consciously, I think. Whereas with people like my sister – who is actually very attractive – but because she's my sister, he wouldn't, he has a very different way of relating to them.

So you didn't feel beautiful.

No. I felt like the cook. I really did. So that was a difficult time. I think actually Nicola was around before I started my training – it was a long time ago, anyway. I think as soon as I started my training, it gave me a glimpse of something I really wanted to do, possibly for the rest of my life, so it was important to me. And it was really difficult.

Did Frank start treating you worse then, or make you feel even dowdier?

No, I don't think so. But although he encouraged me, he was quite resentful. I had to go away for a weekend every month, and he didn't like it. I remember one time I went away, Frank was ill and Diana was looking absolutely like thunder. And I felt so guilty! I thought I ought to be staying at home, looking after these two pathetic creatures. But the moment I reached the motorway, I just thought, thank God I'm away from those two miserable sods!

I know how that feels! [We laugh together.]

And when I was with a group of like-minded individuals, I thought, this is where it's at. Such a relief, unbelievable, to be with a group of people who accepted me as a fellow human being. So that was hard work, but I never regretted it. It was unbelievably hard work – some months I had to write eight essays! Can you imagine, doing eight essays *and* all the cooking here? Sometimes I thought I'd crack up under the strain of it all. That was the point at which Frank got totally obsessed with Mandy. That really did my head in. He actually never had sex with her, because she wouldn't let him. He was really obsessed, I think partly because she wouldn't have sex with him.

So how did you deal with that?

I used to scream a lot. I was in quite a critical bit of my training, trying to work hard, Diana was being extremely demanding, I was trying to cook for all these people, and I had Frank going round like a lovesick teenager, waiting for the telephone to ring. He used to talk about her and write things down, and leave things for me to read. It was all totally maddening.

He didn't feel any need to keep it to himself?

I don't think he could. That's one of the problems. He can't keep things to himself, he always has to tell me. I have said to him, recently, I would rather not know all the details; because when I'm trying to deal with my own life, and trying to do things here, struggling with all that, it is really difficult.

How did you cope?

I think I coped by retreating into my work. I did get pretty mad. Once she rang – he'd been waiting for her to ring for about four days – and I could see him saying, is it her? I snatched the phone and shouted and screamed down the phone at her. I just flipped. I didn't care. He went berserk. He said, 'God, you've really screwed things up now. I was waiting for that phone call, finally she rings and you screamed.'

Then of course I felt dreadful. I felt terribly guilty, I tried to ring her back, I was going to say, oh it's fine.

But it wasn't fine.

It wasn't fine at all! But you know, the usual sort of guilt trip – what have I done, I've made him so miserable, despite the fact that he'd been making me feel miserable for months; that kind of all went out of the window and I just felt awfully guilty.

The contortions we women put ourselves through! For Tessa to feel guilty is absurd – as she now knows – yet this is how she reacts. Like many others who share their lives with difficult men, Tessa is allowing Frank's view of the situation to take precedence over hers.

All through that, you were still in love with Frank?

Yes. That's funny, isn't it. I think there's a very strong part in women that says, if you're with someone, even if you've actually gone off them, if they treat you badly. . . it's odd, women go berserk when men say they'll leave, even if the woman has already decided to leave. But I felt, I still feel, a very strong commitment to Frank and a very strong commitment to making our relationship work. That is because of Diana: I want her to have a stable family. I do see my future with Frank.

Anyway, that was fairly brief – four or five months and it burnt itself out. It was horrendous. I'd say, I'm not going to cook today, and I think people who came here picked up that something was wrong. I think she moved away. He had a couple of other relationships that I knew about; he was having a relationship with a woman in London, but because she lived a long way away I didn't find that so threatening. I'm not actually sure he told me about that.

Then after Mandy, he had a relationship with somebody I knew quite well, another artist. She was modelling for him too. They'd be in that room, just across the corridor. I'd wonder what I was going to hear every time I went past the door. I didn't like her. I was quite upset about that. One time he was driving me somewhere, I just jumped out the car because I couldn't bear it.

How did he deal with you being upset?

He tried not to take any notice, tries to ignore it. He finds it very difficult to look at my pain – it brings up too much stuff for him.

This reluctance to see the effect their behaviour has on the woman with whom they live seems to be common among difficult men. Tessa makes her feelings perfectly clear to Frank, yet he feels free to ignore them.

He goes back to this thing that this is what we agreed, he's a creative person and he needs it.

Because he is an artist, he can't help it?

That's right. I would be blocking his art if I tried to stop it. That brought up a lot for me about my mother dying because she was quite rigid. So when Frank accuses me of things I instantly start thinking I'm getting like my mother.

Does he tell you you're being like your mother?

He has a few times. He knows that really gets to me, it presses all my buttons. Maybe now would be a good time to talk about my mother.

Last July my mother was very ill indeed and was taken into hospital. She stopped eating and I knew she was going to die. She'd looked dreadful for a long time. Nobody really knew – it was slow onset – and then I knew she had cancer. We were incredibly upset about it. I hadn't had a very good relationship with my mother, and suddenly I was being forced to look at my relationship with her because she was about to die.

She got weaker and weaker, she needed a lot of looking after and my dad couldn't cope, so my sister and I made an agreement with my dad that we'd keep her out of hospital because she hated hospitals. One of us would stay, then the other would. The first weekend I went up to look after her, when I came back Mandy was staying. I was really freaked out. That was all very odd, there was a very odd atmosphere in the house. She eventually left after much histrionics. That was when Frank told me he was having a relationship with Anya.

I found that really really difficult. I knew my mother was dying and I'd have to be spending a lot of time there.

You really needed support. It seems that every time you need support, Frank withdraws it.

I think the other thing that's quite important is that Frank's mother died when he was a baby. I have mothered him a lot.

Maybe that's one reason he chose you: because you are that sort of person.

Yes, and I think it's one reason I chose him. Because I like men who are quite stroppy and independent, but I also like to mother them. So Frank was the ideal combination.

Anyway. . . I felt absolutely devastated. I was just in a state. I knew whenever I stayed with my mother, he'd be with Anya. One time they had sex in our bed and that really freaked me out. But even then, I couldn't say it. I couldn't. Because there was all this stuff around my mother dying. I was totally immersed in this stuff with my mother, then I'd come back and there'd be all this going on with Anya here.

Were you also worried about Diana?

Oh yes. She was reacting very badly, being very difficult at school. I was really grief-stricken about Frank and my mother. He said I was projecting my grief about my mother onto him, but that certainly wasn't the whole story. That made me very angry. I was incredibly vulnerable.

Then I had this flash of inspiration that I had to let go of things, let go of my fear. It was part of understanding what my mother needed to do. My mother couldn't let go, she was clinging to life – she was unconscious for nearly two weeks, she didn't eat or drink for ten days, but she wouldn't let go.

This was a crucial turning point for Tessa. She had first offered to record an interview for this book shortly after her mother's death. She had described her insight in general terms: that she had needed to let go of the things that held her back, and open her heart to love. This had been the breakthrough that allowed her to revive her partnership with Frank. At the time I was mystified but intrigued: I knew nothing about Anya, although I had known about Tessa's mother's illness. What had struck me at the time of the telephone call was the transformation in Tessa's voice. The strain and unhappiness, which I had attributed to the stress of looking after her dying mother, had clearly gone.

It really made me think about the triangular situation between me, Frank and Anya. I felt, not that I had to be passive, but that I had to try to dissolve this me being hurt, I had to try and be more open to Anya. So I rang her up and we spent a really nice morning together making bread and jam, and we went for a walk. And I felt OK with her.

Anyway, Anya and I got to know each other quite well and had some good times together. It happened naturally, we just opened up to each other. Then she became just another human being for me, rather than The Other Woman and a total threat.

Frank was really happy about it. He put his arms around both of us and said he wanted us to model together. I felt that would be really good, it would help me to overcome my feeling that I'm not worth painting. so now he's doing a beautiful painting of both of us. I feel really positive about that.

That sounds like Frank saying you're not being discarded.

That's right. I'm really glad we're doing that.

I started telling friends but they weren't any help. They'd all look at me and say, 'You're out of your brain! Tell him to fuck off!' But it's not that easy. As you know! I'd say, what about Diana? It's bloody unhelpful.

Time and again, women who live with difficult men meet this reaction when they try to talk about the problem. Surely their friends must realise that if leaving, or throwing the difficult man out of the marital home were an acceptable option, this is what would be happening?

I just stopped talking to anybody. People thought I was really unfriendly, but if I started talking, I'd start crying. So I'd avoid seeing people. I cut off. One of the hardest things was seeing patients through all of this. Stiff upper lip, keep my tears back. . . But I knew my job was a lifeline. A couple of times a patient would tell me something that was too close to what I was going through and I'd think, I'm going to cry; but I didn't, and I was really pleased that I didn't. It was a real victory, managing to hold it together. Because the last thing you want when you're in distress is for the person you've gone to for help to crack up in front of you. A bit of empathy is fine, but that's all. Then I started seeing this brilliant counsellor.

She's really professional and so clear. She never said leave him, she never said he's a bastard. A couple of times I could see her professional thing slipping, but she never, ever judged. She said, you've just been through so much and you handled it so well. I couldn't have managed without her.

How did you find your counsellor?

Through one of my friends. As soon as I met Sheila, I knew she was somebody I could work with. I knew I could say anything to Sheila. I've only seen her about eight times but it's been enough.

She helped me to understand I needed to be more in touch with myself and that I had to feel good about myself. She helped me to see what was my stuff and what was Frank's stuff, that I had to make boundaries. I had to say what I was prepared to do and what I wasn't prepared to do, and know what I wanted, to be totally clear about what I wanted, what felt OK and what didn't.

The counsellor said I had to be clear about what I would put up with. If I didn't want them to have sex in my bed, if I didn't want her to stay over when I wasn't here, I had to be clear about that. She said, it's your house and your space, and you've got to feel OK there. I had difficulty with that but I worked on it. I catch myself thinking I'm being an uptight neurotic woman, and I say this, and the counsellor asks me, 'Who says you ought to put up with it?' And that's so important, because I have this voice in my head that says you don't want to be like your mother, you've got to be ultimately flexible, you've got to do this. My counsellor said, 'You don't have to do it all, you only have to do what you feel right with.'

I've really learnt an amazing amount about myself through all this. There are still times when I feel wobbly – for example when I come in and find Frank and Anya in a passionate embrace – I feel really left out, as any woman would. You know, she's half my age, and all those old records start to play in my head. But most of the time now, I feel really positive. I feel really good that Frank's doing a painting of both of us. . .

But there are times when she irritates me intensely. . . Diana can't stand her. Diana knows a bit about this because on one occasion when I went to look after my dad after my mother died, Diana was ill. Frank went off to go to bed with Anya and left Diana ill on her own. I just flipped.

His behaviour seems extraordinary sometimes.

Honestly it was one of the worst things. I felt in one sense that I could kill him, because I felt so angry. Diana was so upset and vulnerable and he just buggered off to where Anya lives.

Anyway, it all erupted when I got home and I was angry. That was another thing: telling Frank that's just not on.

Does he accept that?

Yes, he does. But it's constantly shifting. Frank will push the boundaries one way, and I'll push back. . . That's what it's about really, that's what relationships are about, aren't they?

You can't live it all on his terms.

Absolutely. That's what I've learnt. That's the really valuable lesson I've learnt from going to the counsellor. Because she hasn't said, he's a bastard, leave him; she said, what do you need, what are you thinking?

This is the first step away from the role of victim: focusing on what *you* think and what *you* need. Only when you are clear about this can you move towards ensuring that your needs are met. Tessa is not focusing on Frank here, but on herself. Blame, and all the destructive emotions associated with it, becomes irrelevant.

The first few times I saw her, I was just in tears the whole time, I used to just howl. Sometimes I'd hardly stop crying the whole hour. I was so distressed when I started seeing her: my mother was dying and I was in a terrible state. But gradually she helped me to see things clearer, to make boundaries. She said – which was really nice – boundaries don't have to be rigid; why not imagine your boundaries are made of willow, so they're flexible and you can peep over them or through them, or hide behind them if you want. They're nice and bendy but they protect you as well. Like hedges instead of walls.

A friend wouldn't be able to say that. She said, you're sur-rounded by people who say, he's this and he's that, and you don't want to hear that at the moment because it's not helpful. You need to get in touch with what you need. And you're saying very clearly, you don't want to leave, you want to make it work. There are still days when I wish he didn't have a girlfriend, but he will never say he will stop seeing Anya. He says, you married me and you knew what I was like, and I'll probably stay like this till I die.

And that's the truth.

That is the truth, and he doesn't flinch from telling me. I just hope that as he gets older they'll get fewer. But I've learnt I'm strong enough to cope. I've been through my mother dying and what is quite a serious relationship for him. And I've survived.

AMANDA

Amanda wears no makeup, her hair is long and unstyled. She belongs to the 'alternative' society, a loose group of people who try to live in ways that they feel are more ethical than the mainstream, rejecting materialism and the consumer society. Rather than accept conventional answers, she tries to think through her situation and come up with a novel solution. But the emotions with which she struggles will be familiar to women whose lifestyles are totally different from hers.

We've been together seventeen years; I'm forty-four now. We were both adults when this relationship began. It was Chris's first serious relationship and I'd never lived with anybody before; it was quite new, quite fiery, exciting at first. And it was sudden: it didn't take long to get to know each other. We were travelling abroad during the courtship period and it was intense. It was love, passion.

We were brought together by advertisements: we both advertised for somebody to go travelling with. Our first child was born two years after we came back. The commitment was there; she was planned.

Do you feel the commitment is still there? Whatever the problems now, you both want to save the family unit?

Yes, that's true for both of us. We just come from incredibly different places. Chris is having a relationship with another woman, Julie. He talks of her as a very close friend. She is not a wife, and though the relationship has a sexual element, it's really a friendship. Conventionally, they are lovers, but that's not how he looks at it.

If it were a close friendship without the sexual element, could you accept it?

Yes. I could. At first it was a close friendship without the sex, but really it's been sexual from the beginning although they didn't consummate it. That was two years ago. They started sleeping together about a year ago. It was all hard, from the beginning. It's the sexual side that really hurts.

Chris seeks to confound Amanda and reduce the legitimacy of her feelings about his relationship with Julie by persuading her that what she knows to be true is not true. He and Julie are lovers, but because 'that's not how he looks at it', Amanda feels she should react as though he is not being unfaithful. She is confronting two unacceptable options: either Chris is being dishonest and she cannot trust him, or she cannot trust the evidence of her own senses. The former option seriously threatens the values that underpin the relationship; the second throws her into a sort of limbo where she cannot believe her own perceptions and must be led by Chris. Amanda seems to prefer to go along with Chris's way of seeing the situation – but to do so, she must sacrifice her own grip on reality.

Is it the first time this has happened, the first time he's had a sexual relationship with another woman?

Yes.

And this wasn't part of any agreement between you? You didn't have, in any sense, an open relationship?

No. No.

So he's broken his part of the deal, hasn't he?

He says he's changed. He's not the person I married. His needs – he's discovered more. Yes, conventionally, he has broken his side . . . but he's never lied to me about it.

This perception of Chris as someone who never lies is very important to Amanda. But at what point does distortion of the truth become a lie?

> He's been completely and utterly open. Because we lived with the other family. . . it's not that he used to disappear. He would say he was going to see Julie.

Was she a close friend of yours?

> No, it was just the family we shared with. Two families. We got on well, we had lots in common. But she wasn't special to me. She was having a hard time with her husband, and Chris was her knight in shining armour.

Do you feel she would like to take Chris away from you?

> No. She's not a threat in that sense. They don't want to live together. Julie's very happy with the way things are. And of course that makes me very cross, because she's got it all ways. She's got Chris, she's got her freedom. She can do what she likes.

I don't blame you for feeling cross! You seem to imagine you should be quite saintly!

> Yes, but you see, what I find is really hard is that we have very strong feelings between us, Chris and I. If I couldn't bear the sight of him, or he drove me mad, it would be easy because I could just say, sod it, and I'd be off. But we have a lot of love, a lot of affection. We just love being together. You know, it's not an easy thing to give that up. A lot of people in faithful relationships don't have that. I have a happy home. What do I do? Do I go for principle?

So what's the principle?

> That he should be faithful to me, he should not have a sexual relationship with another woman.

Because you find that intolerable.

> I find that dreadful. Well, it's funny, before they started sleeping together, that sexual act had such huge importance, it was a

huge fear. I don't know whether I'm making a mountain out of a molehill, hanging onto conventional morals, you know.

Up to that point, I thought, if that happens, that's it. Then when I discovered it had happened, I said, right, that's it, finished. But I couldn't do it. We are still together.

And you're not about to split up.

No. But it seems – what is difficult is what I feel are his demands – He says they aren't demands, they're needs that he specifies – are getting more and more and more. They're coming on me, more and more. I feel suffocated by his demands. If we could just have a certain clear understanding.

What about your needs? How do they come into this?

I get confused about my needs. And he's very clear on his needs. He keeps asking what my needs are, but I'm very foggy on them. When I come to think of it, my needs are that he should do this and he should do that, and I can see that that's not the way. I just don't know what to do about it.

Amanda is having difficulty separating her personal needs from the relationship. Until she becomes clear about what she will tolerate and what she will not, she will continue to be vulnerable to the expansion of Chris's 'needs' and a diminishing sense of legitimacy of her feelings.

As a couple, we are very interested in the spiritual side of life, not just the material side. Spiritual growth is very important to us.

I suspect that Amanda views self-sacrifice as a virtue. In order to deal with her sense that Chris doesn't care enough about her to spare her this pain, she struggles to improve her own self-image by behaving with total equanimity, smiling gently like the Buddha and somehow being above it all. If she were not so earthbound, she would be able to distance herself from pain.

Do you mean you feel you're blocked in your growth?

No, I feel I'm being helped in my growth. It's bloody painful growth.

It usually is!

I am becoming aware of patterns that I've hung onto from childhood. Slightly spoilt behaviour. If things don't go my way, I can go into a tantrum. That is being squashed.

What, just recently?

This has been a pattern in my life. I like attention and I like to be special and wanted, and all these things.

Don't we all!

But I've been too sensitive to things; I always was as a child. I can see that now. I should have left those sort of feelings behind in my adult life. I think this is part of learning to deal with it. I do believe and trust that Chris is committed. I feel confident that we could stay together if I can cope.

It sounds as though you're expected to make all the compromises.

That is how I feel. But Chris has not been sailing through this feeling wonderful, although it does seem like that to everybody else. They think, he's getting his cake and eating it. Conventionally, that is the picture. I don't feel that is the case. If I did, I wouldn't have stuck it out.

I wonder what would drive Amanda away? She seems to allow the boundaries of what is acceptable to move at Chris's instigation, as he discovers new 'needs'. She did not leave when confronted with behaviour that she had earlier seen as beyond limits.

But I still find it bloody difficult, I still sink back into conventional thinking and wish it wasn't happening.

Amanda's desire to junk *'conventional thinking'* adds to the problem. She feels unable to trust her thinking, her feelings, or her perception. This appears to me to be a very dangerous situation, one which could lead to a serious mental breakdown. But because Amanda sees it as an opportunity for *'spiritual growth'*, she insists on remaining within this relationship.

Conventional thinking and spiritual growth are parts of a value structure within which Chris is able to manipulate Amanda, so that if she doesn't like something, there's something wrong with her or her value judgements: there's nothing wrong with the value structure.

> It isn't comfortable for him. He is suffering. I do trust him on that one. We are both working through a lot of stuff, you know. I don't go off and live it up when they're together. We've sat for hours in a car park trying to sort something out. He says he'd love it if I could come and be part of it, be with them. But I can't.

Amanda appears to believe that because Chris is 'suffering', just as she is, she must seek to ease his pain. He offers her a way out – the ultimate self-sacrifice: 'come and be part of it' (although there's no suggestion that Julie wants this). This would mean that Amanda would have to deny her feelings totally.

He's like a spider, wrapping her up in this tangled web. She seems able to hang on to her sense of individuality just enough to resist.

> If they were sitting having coffee, I couldn't just go and join them. I can't do that. I have a tendency to isolate myself. If I feel two people are getting on really well, I think, they don't want me. I see that pattern throughout my life. I have too much pride.

Don't you think pride is necessary to maintain your strength, so you can go forward?

> No, because if you can let go of things like pride, it's a much bigger leap forward in self-worth. I don't know, really.

I feel that when I have less pride, I function less well.

> Pride can be different things. It can be positive, but it can be quite negative. Stubborn pride. I don't mean self-worth, that's really necessary, I mean thinking you are better than somebody else.

How do you feel about yourself?

> I think I feel fine on that level. I have self-worth, I'm good at that. I am the breadwinner of the family – I'm the person who

claims family credit. Chris is the househusband. In practice, we both do whatever we can do to earn money for the family. He does as much, in a way, as I do.

It sounds as though you feel there's a good balance in your household, in everyday things.

Yes. There is. That's right. He keeps questioning me about how I feel about the value of our time together, because I can get carried away with them two, the jealousy. He does cooking more than I do, he looks after the house very well and he is very supportive to me in my work. We do have a good solid sort of home. When I feel low, I say, but it's just bloody domestic arrangements, nothing exciting! You go swanning off here, there and everywhere with Julie. And he says, it's only because I haven't got any other choice. She can't come to the house. We have to go somewhere.

Amanda's sense of self-worth appears to be bound up with conformity to the structure of values that imprisons her. While she fits in with the requirements of these values, she feels worthwhile. The more tightly bound she becomes, the more valuable she may feel.

Do you feel that there's a whole part of him that you're not connecting with – like he's taking part of himself away from you?

I could make it that way, but that would come from me and not from him.

I sense that anything that comes from Amanda is perceived as less valuable as something coming from Chris. This underwrites my above view, of her perception of her self-worth.

He would share with me what he does with Julie. He would tell me where they went. I don't want to know. I shut myself away from it because it hurts. I don't think they do anything really exciting. Just go where they can. It is a part of our life that I'm not a part of, but that's my choice. My defence.

You keep saying it's your reaction that's unacceptable. Somehow you've got to learn to react differently; then it would be all right.

I wish I didn't have it. Chris keeps saying, what do you want? In theory I can see that love is OK. I can't see any reason to stop somebody loving somebody else. Because I can't see any logical reason why not. Except I feel threatened by it. Because it's what we are desperately trying to teach our children: to love each other. And there's me saying, 'I don't want you to love her.' I can't logically give a reason why not.

Amanda seems to believe that her emotional reactions must be logically defensible: this would make them (in theory) acceptable to Chris. Her loss of trust in her own feelings and perceptions has undermined her ability to be honest about herself. She is not able to say, this is how I feel and the way I feel should be important in itself. Emotions are rarely logical; they are about how we feel, not how we think. Amanda spends too much time examining her feelings rather than acknowledging and acting on them.

So there's a conflict within you.

There is a conflict in me. About how much I can humanly bear and accept and enjoy. Because of the frantic fear, you know, in myself. I can't bear the idea of them making love. I shut it out. It frightens me to death.

Chris and I still make love the way we've always made love, with great care. . . It isn't in any way diminished because he happens to make love to somebody else. It's a different relationship. Why should it diminish our love? I can see the logic in that, but it makes me freak. It makes me withdraw.

Group love only works when everybody involved is happy about it. Anyone who is not happy gets driven out – and this is what is happening to Amanda. Her sense of threat is entirely justified.

If you have children, you have one child and you love that child. Then if you have another child, you don't love the first child any less. Your love grows to encompass the other child. He just loves another woman too, in a different way. Why should that diminish. . . He says he loves me more, now, but I find that hard to accept. I still feel challenged and threatened and competitive.

Amanda's instinct is absolutely correct. What Chris says is unacceptable. If he loved her and was aware of her feelings, and he loved the other woman, he would have to choose between them.

It's not just a matter of coping. I can't cope. But it shouldn't be a matter of coping. I don't want to live my life coping. I want to live my life fully.

Have you tried living apart?

Yes. Chris went away for eight weeks. But he was just in the next village and continued to come to see me – in fact, perhaps we saw too much of each other, because I was quite enjoying being on my own! We've always been under each other's feet, neither of us has ever gone out to work since we've been living together, and the children don't go to school so they're with us all the time. So we've had quite an intense life, really.

Such constant closeness can make it difficult for a woman to retain a strong sense of self. Amanda is always under Chris's influence.

I said one of my needs was that I needed to know specific times when he would be around.

Here she is trying to gain some sense of predictability so that she can have control over part of her life.

I do need my own space, but I don't want to go to bed on my own every night. I haven't specified time when I want to be alone, just when he's going to be with me.

I would like to be able to share this with people, but I can't tell anybody, really. Whoever I tell, they can't believe that I'm still there. They can't support Chris. It's not empowering to me, when people say I should leave him. I don't want to be a victim and I don't feel that I am. I feel quite strong and positive.

It seems to me that Amanda has very little power within this relationship. What she describes as feeling 'strong and positive' is not what I can recognise as such. What she sees as strength seems to be her attachment to the values that are causing such pain in this relationship.

There is a certain core of people who are supportive, they love Chris and they can see there's a lot between us. But they find it hard to see me going through such pain without feeling angry towards Chris and I don't really want people to be angry towards Chris. He's not unkind to me, he's not violent. He's very kind and very loving and very supportive and he's never hit me – though I've hit him. He's never even raised his voice to me. Nothing like that. How can I hate him for loving another woman? If he did hit me or shut me out, I'd have something to grab hold of. Obviously I'm glad he isn't like that. He is difficult too, a know-it-all man, but God, nobody's perfect!

What you see is a loving man, whom you love.

Whom I love. And who loves me and loves the children.

A year after I taped this interview, I spoke to Amanda again. Nothing had basically changed. She continues to believe that she should regard Chris's relationship with Julie as an opportunity for personal growth and development, but finds this ideal difficult to achieve. '*It's less traumatic,*' she told me, '*Though it isn't changed.*'

I'm feeling more settled. I was left some money when a relative died, so we've bought a house and I've got a base and that helps. I'm continually changing, working on becoming more secure in myself, but when I'm feeling vulnerable I don't feel secure – it flies out the window.

Chris still has a very strong relationship with Julie. He doesn't want to move out. Sometimes I wonder if it's worth it – Chris is no god sent from above – but actually I'm learning quite a lot: strength and openness. I don't want to run away from it. Chris says he feels I'm blocking it, turning my back on his relationship with Julie. He feels it would be more helpful to him if I accepted it.

This is a man who wants it all his own way – and will tie Amanda into knots to achieve it. He manipulates her, presenting his 'needs' as reasonable while her feelings are unreasonable; and she responds by struggling to fit his picture of a good woman.

I am getting to accept it more; he spends the night with her sometimes and I don't shiver or fly into a rage. But I don't want to see her or talk to her.
In the end I'm sure my life would be a lot easier if I could meet her and feel OK – but I panic at the thought of meeting her. Seeing them together still hurts. Maybe one day I'll feel strong enough in myself that it won't hurt. I can see that if I was in his situation, I'd want that too.

Still she sees her life in terms of his, subordinating her needs, desires and feelings to his.

I feel quite strong though I go up and down like a yo-yo – I feel hopeless and a failure sometimes. I do feel good in myself at the moment.

MARIAN

When Marian opened her door to me, I saw a delicate, rather sad-looking woman. I knew nothing about her, her life, or the nature of the difficulties with which she was, or had been, living; all she had told me was that she was willing to talk and that she had a story that she thought would interest me. Her house was rich with paintings, sculptures, *objets d'art*, many amusing pieces that I would love to own. She introduced me to her husband, Ted, who retired discreetly to another room.

How long have you known Ted?

She spoke slowly, quietly, hesitating frequently.

> Twenty years this year. We met when I was a student at the local art school and Ted was teaching. But for at least three years before that, when I was at sixth form college, I used to see him getting onto the bus. He always wore a very distinctive coat with an enormous fur collar and he walked with a stick, and I used to wonder about him. So I observed him at a distance for quite a long time.

You'd been watching him.

> Yes, from when I was about seventeen.

Had you had any serious, committed relationships before this one?

> The relationship with Ted only really began when I was twenty-one. Prior to that, I'd had a boyfriend since I was sixteen. We got engaged, went through all the usual – expectations, I suppose, of other people. Didn't think too much of myself.

Thinking little of one's self seems to be a hallmark of a potential victim.

> We were planning to get married. Then when I went to art school at eighteen, that was a big turning point. It just opened up such a treasure box of different types of people from all walks of life.

That was an exciting time. We're talking about the mid-seventies, when there was still a lot of optimism around.

> Yes, there was. And I was doing what I wanted to do and I met lots of new people. I realised for the first time that the thoughts that I had were not unusual. Lots of people thought the same way as myself. About all sorts of things, down to fairly trivial things. Like I used to feel very awkward about New Year's Eve. I discovered

that lots of other people felt the same way, I wasn't different. I don't think I'd had the opportunity before to talk about what made me tick, even with my family, because I come from a working-class family who are very limited in terms of intellect.

It sounds like a really exciting and happy time.

It was. But to put this into a broader context, I think it's important that you know that throughout my teenage years I was abused at home.

This is a totally unexpected revelation. But it explains why it was so important to Marian that she should be normal, not 'different'.

Sexually abused?

Yes. Yes. From the age of twelve until I was. . . I actually didn't get any respite from it until I was almost twenty-three. That's had an enormous influence on the way I was then and the way I am now. That part of my life I think is still causing me problems now, and the fact that I've never opened up properly about it I think is a big problem. And that's created added difficulties for any relationships I might have. I can't make any judgements about any relationship without using that as a starting point. Because I don't know how I would have been without that.

I can talk about it reasonably openly with people that I trust, but I haven't ever really explored it in any serious depth. It's much too painful.

Have you had any counselling or psychotherapy?

No. Absolutely nothing. I made a conscious decision at the age of seventeen that it wasn't going to affect me.

If only such wishes could come true! Marian has already made it clear that the abuse affected her profoundly.

I can remember the moment when I thought about it, when I thought about the psychological pain, the emotional pain that I'd gone through for a long time, and was very disturbed about how it might affect me sexually, how it might affect me if I had children of my own – all sorts of things. But they were very private thoughts. I didn't discuss them with anybody.

The first time I ever revealed any of it was when I was sixteen, to my eldest sister. I've never explored since, with that sister or my other sister, what effect that had on them.

Were they abused too?

I think so. Certainly there's one occasion that I know of, one of my sisters revealed that something had happened to her. My other sister's a closed book, but I'm very suspicious that something happened to her too, because I don't think it could have not happened to her. She's never, ever talked about it. I don't think she ever will. But there are some things, some parts of her behaviour, that I recognise.

Ted, of course, knows about all of this. Occasionally we talk about it. Any other relationship, I think I use that one as a measure. I decided, whatever happened in my life, like the pain of somebody dying or a difficult close relationship, nothing could be worse than what I'd gone through. That was how I actually coped.

Using such a dire standard of comparison would make almost anything seem acceptable. Marian seems to be saying that she *decided* she would tolerate abusive relationships.

What made it so bad for you?

It wasn't the physical abuse itself. It was the torment, the psychological torment of not knowing, day to day, whether something was going to happen.

And you dreaded it.

Absolutely. Every day. Absolutely every day. It was just constant fear. Having no form of escape. When I went to art school, for the first time I did feel some form of escapism. I was with very kind, very open-minded people.

You continued to live at home?

Yes.

You couldn't see a way out?

Not at that time, no.

After I spoke with you on the phone a couple of weeks ago, I did sit and think about it quite a lot. I couldn't not reveal these things because they are so significant in my life. I wouldn't be who I am now without having gone through all of that. It's still difficult, because my family don't live far away. Coping with Ted – all those sorts of things – somehow they were secondary, because I'd had to live with that every day for a long, long time. Sexual abuse has become much more open now, with Childline.

Nobody talked about it at all then, did they? You must have felt totally isolated.

Oh, totally isolated. In the long term, I think it's affected me in that I'm not a good communicator, I don't socialise easily. Through those formative years, I did just isolate myself totally from school age. I can remember being talked about by other groups of girls at school because I was so quiet and withdrawn.

You weren't part of the group.

No. I survived by withdrawing, by retreating inside my own head. I've reflected on it, of course, many many times, wondered if I should have counselling. On good days, I think oh, I can handle all that, but there are still weak moments. It's still very painful. But Ted helped me to put all of that into perspective and to talk about it. He didn't over-react, he was able to stay objective about it most of the time. Certainly when I first met him he was. He put it into some sort of context.

Whilst it was very difficult to deal with – you felt the whole range of emotions from extreme anger to pain, you know, a deep deep sadness – I was able to step back from it and think, this person's got a real problem.

So you always saw it as your father's problem. You didn't blame yourself.

I think I did when I was very young. At twelve years old I was still a child. I had no idea what was going on. I didn't know what was acceptable and what wasn't. I knew that it felt wrong for me. I knew there was a problem there.

There was a chap called Ray Wire – I've seen him quite a lot on television over the years – and I think when I was about eighteen I saw him on television and he was talking about sexual abuse in families. Talking about the victim and the perpetrator. It was the first time I'd ever heard anyone explain it, how the – whoever actually does the abusing – how they always blame the victim, the child, whoever it might be. And in fact that's absolutely wrong. It's always the other way around. They make excuses for themselves. And. . . like I say, I've heard this chap quite a lot over the years and I do realise these people have got a serious problem.

The other thing I did was make myself uglier. I thought that physically there must be some reason why this was happening to me. It must be to do with my shape or my face. So I purposely stayed very thin. I was much thinner then than I am now. And I didn't smile a lot – I find that difficult, even now, to smile. I did absolutely withdraw, certainly during the teenage years.

When I was around twenty-one, the pressure wasn't quite as bad because I was learning to get it into perspective. I was becoming an adult, I suppose, about it all. So maybe the stress wasn't as obvious then. But certainly it was when I was at school. I can remember going to grammar school and within the first month, I got shingles. This was when the abuse started, at exactly the same time as me going to grammar school. The rash was all around my groin, and my periods had started as well, all those all at the same time. I remember having to show my mum this painful rash, and the doctor diagnosed shingles. He was very surprised that someone so young had got that problem.

So it was quite significant, really, at the age eleven and a half, my periods starting, and the abuse starting, and going to grammar school. I found it quite difficult to maintain concentration. I don't think I did myself justice at school. I don't think I gave my best at that time. I struggled through school, I only came out with four O levels. The one area I was always strong in was art.

Did art help you to deal with what was going on?

I think so, because it's such a private expression of who you are and what you want to do. It's actually very relaxing. It's about being withdrawn, then getting it out on paper. But I think I had a lot more potential at a young age than came out. That's what I think at forty, anyway. It feels like I'm just growing up. I feel like I've missed a big chunk somewhere.

Because you were forced into becoming suddenly adult at eleven, when you were still a child.

Yes.

Can we go back, to when you met Ted, how that happened and how your relationship developed?

Ted at that time was quite a womaniser. He certainly had a strong reputation within the art school. There were a couple of students that I knew about, and another couple who'd left or moved on, all very attractive women. I found him quite charming. He had a very good sense of humour. I never saw myself as attractive at that time; quite serious, intense, quite skinny as well. Not very open. I used to watch and observe what went on.

I'd had this long-term relationship with someone else and I knew it wasn't right. I was getting married in order to leave home. I knew that that was why I was doing it, not because I wanted to spend the rest of my life with that person. And I decided I couldn't do that, I couldn't live with myself if I continued with it. So I let that relationship drift.

When I was a student, people would go to the pub in groups. Ted would go, and there was another friend who was very very supportive, and we used to go to the pub regularly, and parties, and it just gradually developed. But at that time I certainly didn't foresee any long-term relationship with Ted at all. There was a sexual attraction there, certainly on my part. I definitely chased him, it wasn't the other way around.

So your experience of abuse didn't put you off men.

Oh no, I don't think it did. But I was also fascinated by his intellect. I hadn't talked to anyone, ever, before, where I really respected their knowledge and their view of the world and I was fascinated by that. I was really interested in what he had to say and his perspective on the world. It wasn't just sex, it was a lot more than that. I enjoyed listening to him. He was a natural teacher. So the attraction was definitely to do with that as well.

At that time I knew he was married, he'd got two children; I think his daughter was about ten and his son about twelve, so I knew I was on pretty dodgy ground with all of that. And I didn't want to cause any serious pain. But he'd always told me that he had a very open relationship with Pauline, his wife, and that she had relationships too, with other men. I was never quite convinced, I have to admit, that it wasn't painful to either of them. I was never really sure what was going on.

Did you know her as well?

Certainly, I'd met her.

Once more, this interview takes a turn that surprises me. I realise that the other woman in this relationship is in fact Ted's ex-wife.

Did she know you and Ted were lovers?

Oh yes, she did. But he was very loyal to his family. He always used to go home, he'd make sure they were clothed and fed – all the basic things. He says he feels very guilty about the lack of attention he paid to his children. But I observed him paying a lot of attention to them. He was a lot more attentive than my family had been, my father.

So we both had different perspectives on that relationship and we still disagree about it, even now. He certainly did love Pauline, there's no doubt about that at all, but that relationship was under a lot of strain long before I came on the scene. She had another man a long time before, which I'm sure did disturb him quite a lot, from observing his body language if I talk about it. He denies that but I still think it bothers him.

So I don't absolutely trust his view on that relationship. I think he always thought his relationship with Pauline would end, and had for a long time. But with the children, there's a responsibility. He wouldn't have ever pulled out on that. He actually finds the idea of having created two human beings very difficult to handle. He doesn't find those relationships easy either.

That's caused difficulties in our relationship, because when I talk about children. . . He certainly never wanted to have any more. It's been another area that's been very difficult for me, because ten years ago, I did. There again, I think many women feel that in their late twenties, early thirties, the biological clock, all that sort of stuff. And my feelings about that fluctuate quite a lot. I'm forty-one years old now, I don't think I would seriously consider having children at this age, but I found Ted's reaction to my talking about it very difficult to handle. It's always been an absolute no-go area. Right the way through the relationship.

Marian speaks quietly about things that matter to her. Ted may not have realised the intensity of her feelings; and how important children are to her.

This quiet intensity is probably one of the results of the abuse she suffered as a child.

I made my mind up that when I left art school, the relationship would stop. That it would have to, because he was married. I made my mind up that that would be the end of it.

At that stage, were you in love with him?

Oh, I think so, yes.

How did you make that decision? Was it connected with your feelings about yourself, maybe that you didn't deserve to have what you wanted?

I think that was true. I thought that Ted still loved his wife and his family. I think I deceived him and I deceived myself for a long time. I knew that he was very, very important to me.

Marian was actively suppressing her knowledge of what was important to her, failing to acknowledge her own feelings. This is likely to be the way she handled the psychological suffering caused by the abuse during her teenage years.

*So you weren't letting him know how important he was, because
you didn't want to take him away from his wife and family.*

No, I didn't reveal any of my true feelings at that time. I just
decided that that would be the end of the relationship. I remember leaving the art school and thinking, what am I going to
do now? I'd bought a little terraced house with the chap I'd
been planning to marry, and that was standing there empty, no
decision had been made as to what to do with it.

I took a job by the seaside, worked in a hotel for the summer.
Because I'd come from a close-knit family, that went completely
against the grain.

This family is not close-knit – not if individuals within it
feel unable to talk about issues that are desperately important to
them. It is tightly bound. Escape from its clutches is very difficult.

I'd been on holiday there, so I just rang up the job centre there,
they gave me a list of hotels and I kept phoning till I got a job.
All of that was very, very pleasant, it was the first time I felt
totally free. Free of the problems at home, and able to get the
relationship with Ted into perspective, and even able to accept
that it had come to its natural end and that I wouldn't reflect on
it in a negative way. I'd had some very, very happy times and it
was time to move on.

*You were very philosophical, then. I can imagine that many people
would have been shouting and weeping and railing against their
fate. . . You weren't like that at all. You were determined to cope, to
come to terms with whatever happened to you.*

I actually got involved with a chap when I was there. Only very
briefly, I knew that was a holiday romance. That was only the
third sexual relationship I'd ever had. I felt a great sense of freedom: I was able to sleep at night, totally relaxed, I could switch
off. I remember my sister coming to see me, she said it was
the healthiest she'd ever seen me. That did change me again,
significantly.

When the season came to an end, there were no jobs, so I
came back home.

You went back to your parents' home?

I had to, there was no alternative.

Back to the abuse?

Well, back to the threat of it. By that time the actual abuse had stopped. But there was the fear of it.

After so many years at college and a summer away, it seems unlikely that Marian really had no alternative to returning to her parents' home. That *she* could see no alternative is very different from there being no alternative in fact. The intensity of her painful memories may have focused her mind on the place where she was abused, to the exclusion of other possibilities.

So I decided to go to the previous boyfriend and ask, look, can I go and live in that terraced house? There was quite a lot of work still needed doing on it, bare walls and such, so I said I would do that and I would pay the mortgage. He agreed so I moved in. I suppose I'd got a grip, then, on my life and what I was going to do.

The other thing that happened was, the day I got back from Cornwall, literally the same day, I got a phone call asking me to come for interview for a job. The next week, I got that job.

I went back to the art school to see everybody, because I'd got lots of friends there. As soon as I saw Ted, that was it. There was a moment then when I knew it hadn't ended at all. From that point it did develop quite seriously. I continued to see Ted and I have done ever since.

I would see him about twice a week. It doesn't seem much, in retrospect, but it was, given the commitments he had – a full-time job, a wife, children who needed to be taken to places in the evenings. At that time I was quite happy for it to continue like that because I still felt that he was worth it. But it was painful, very difficult for me when I didn't see him and when he went away on family holidays, that sort of thing. There have been many ups and downs, but it was a very happy time till I was about twenty-seven, twenty-eight.

What happened then?

Well, Pauline had a long-term relationship with a chap called Sam who didn't live far away. The children were growing up, the oldest was already away at college. Ted was always saying as soon as the kids were away, their relationship would dissolve. But then she became ill. The truth was, she had been ill for a long time but Ted wasn't taking it seriously. He didn't realise that psychiatric nurses were going round once a week to give her injections. He thought her behaviour was odd, but because he was out all day, he never actually saw it going on. He knew she'd been to the doctor and she'd been acting strangely. In truth, she'd been a bit bizarre for years but he'd just thought it was Pauline.

But it was getting worse and worse. She used to phone me as well at that time and describe all sort of bizarre situations, things like she'd taken her daughter to hospital to see a specialist, and there was another couple dressed up as them, sat in front of them in the queue. She was so convincing, we'd have these long, long conversations. Ted thought it was strange. It went on for about two years before she was diagnosed as schizophrenic. And of course her relationship with Sam completely broke down.

I'd just bought this house when Ted came and told me Pauline wanted him to sleep with her again. I was incredibly upset. I got very, very angry and very hurt, because for a long time I'd been led to believe that relationship was going to dissolve. But at that point what he was doing was exactly the opposite. And I thought I could no longer continue. I felt resentful that I'd given up so much, I'd put everything into this relationship and was getting very little in return.

We were actually in this room. It was full of furniture, all piled up because I'd literally only just moved in. I threw a photograph down on the floor – a photograph of him – and broke it. That was the first time I'd ever revealed all the pain it was causing me. I don't think I'd ever truly been open with Ted. I'd never revealed just what I did think about him. But I couldn't understand what on earth was going on, and how he could say something like that to me without thinking that it would cause me a lot of distress.

For a long time I think I hadn't been facing up to who I am. That I am a normal woman, and I do have those feelings. And I did feel jealous. But I'd just tripled my mortgage, so I withdrew into myself and threw myself into doing the house for at least two years.

Ted still used to pop round and tell me all his troubles. When he realised how upset I was, I said, well how can you do that? He said, she only wants to sleep with me for comfort. And I couldn't handle that. I said I couldn't deal with that and I wasn't prepared to continue with that.

Although Marian may well have said – and felt – these things, her actions are not consistent with them. In fact, she does continue with the relationship, very much on Ted's terms. And she deals with the pain it causes her in precisely the same way as she had dealt with the distress of her father's abuse – by withdrawing.

The other thing that happened was, he bought a house nearer to town. I saw that as a signal that he was re-setting up home.

So his life was still with Pauline and his children – even though they were leaving home – and you were just the one on the side?

That's right.

This was after eight years or more?

Yes, nine, ten years. And it wasn't what I wanted. There was an occasion when I was twenty-eight, when he asked me if I'd ever wanted children. I found it very difficult to talk to him about that, but I thought he'd picked up on my emotions. I thought, he does understand, he knows I have those feelings. But in fact I'd completely misread it. I thought he might want that too. I thought what he was saying was that he wanted a permanent relationship with me and a family with me, but I was completely wrong.

Here is the crux of the difficulty with Ted: he appears to understand Marian's feelings but at crucial times it becomes clear that he either does not actually understand, or chooses not to acknowledge their significance. Understanding Marian's needs is fine until it requires some commitment from him. Sadly, the trust that was so important to Marian is now wearing thin.

If I try to talk to him about this, he has a completely different view of it. And that's why the relationship now is still very difficult. In fact I think we don't communicate as well now as we did ten, fifteen years ago. I think I've withdrawn the emotional side of myself. It's very deeply hidden.

Having said that, I've never been 100 per cent certain about whether I actually wanted a family. The fear was that I might end up abusing my children because of my history. You hear about that sort of thing, the abused becomes the abuser. So those fears have always been with me.

Ted gets very angry now when I talk about the past. He only wants me to think forwards and I understand why, what he's saying, but sometimes I feel I need to revisit the past in order to try and understand what I'm doing now.

So that you can move on.

That's right. If he'd left home and moved in with me, I'd have wanted a conventional family. When he bought the house with Pauline, the signal I got then was that he was re-creating the family base.

Ted was living two completely separate lives then. I knew him for ten years before I was formally introduced to his children. It was hard. Hard with friends and colleagues at work. But somehow it seems to have quite a lot to do with me. I think in a way it was important for me to survive by myself.

Because of my background, it was a great relief to me to be able to sleep at night. I still remember going to bed the first night in my own house, and not being afraid. Not feeling afraid that someone might come to the room. Not having to almost suffocate myself under pillows, blankets, as I'd done from when I was twelve years old.

So you'd found your strength on your own, when you were safe on your own. That was important to you. Maybe this sort of relationship, where you had to be self-supporting, wasn't as hard for you as it might have been for someone with a different sort of background.

Had Marian chosen this sort of difficult man – or at least tolerated her part in his dual life – because the relationship allowed her the control over her personal life which was so important to her?

I think that's true, yes. I had to assert myself, find out who I was. There was such an enormous chunk of life missing. I can pinpoint different things during my teenage years, but generally I've blanked it out. I have to really work at thinking about the good things that happened then, because it feels like a vacuum, totally withdrawing inside myself. The happiest times were when I was with groups of people when I was a student, then going to Cornwall.

The relationship with Ted did have some very happy moments, but it also had some very painful bits. Waiting for the phone to ring. Waiting for him to turn up, and then when he didn't turn up, not being sure what was really going on. I never quite believed him.

Here the main problem appears to be that Marian has no control over the situation. Such lack of control over the way a man's life interacts with hers is potentially very dangerous to her.

How much was this uncertainty because he wasn't telling you enough?

I think you've hit the nail on the head. I don't think he did tell me everything. There's one particular occasion – which he totally denies – but for me, I know I'm reporting accurately. One Saturday evening we'd been out for a drink and we got back to my house, and sometimes he would stay all night if it was a weekend. This was very deep into that relationship. I can remember him walking into the room. When I walked back, he was leaning with his head in his hands. I asked what was wrong. He wouldn't say and I kept probing because I knew there was a problem. He turned to me and he said he was still in love with Pauline, but she didn't love him. And there was such clarity about what he said.

For me, of course, that was devastating. It came quite out of the blue. And if I mention that now – and I've gone back to it many times, to try and be honest and open about it – he still denies it. He denies that he ever said it.

Did he say that he was in love with you?

Yes. The first time he ever said he loved me was when I was twenty-six. But that was much later. And I truly think that was one of the moments in his life when he was being completely honest. I didn't condemn him for it; in some ways it was a relief to me that he actually said it. I felt that he was revealing to me that he couldn't handle Pauline seeing somebody else, but of course, it just added to my confusion.

It sounds to me as though he did love you, but he also loved Pauline. Both, concurrently.

I think that was true. But I don't think I'd ever get him to admit it. Not now.

But he was saying, at that time, that he wasn't sleeping with Pauline, the relationship was dying, and all that.

Yes. Oh yes.

You don't believe that was true.

That's right. Things didn't match up, didn't marry, somehow. The words that he said didn't match the way he behaved. And again, that caused great confusion for me. But I suppose I must have thought it was worth carrying on.

Confusion, for you, is part of the pattern, isn't it?

Absolutely. I comforted myself by saying none of this was as bad as what I tolerated at home.

I can see it made sense for you to want to have the certainty and security of your own house, your job. . . there's nobody else involved, you're in control and there's no confusion.

That's right. This was how I coped. I needed some form of stability. Even when I bought this house, I spent a lot of time fiddling about with it, making it my own environment. Again, that was a way of surviving, my way of handling it, getting some control. To some people it seems a bit bizarre, the amount of time I spend at home, but to me it's a comfort to sit in my own space and not fear what's round the corner.

There hasn't been fear with Ted, though, except that he might not be there for you.

Oh no, he's a very kind person. When he realised how seriously ill Pauline was, he was spending three nights a week here, that was how he coped with it. But he was still very caring to Pauline, made sure she got all the help she needed. But she eventually moved away.

And that was the point at which Ted moved in with you, when you and he became the family?

Yes. He decided to explore the possibility of early retirement on the grounds of ill health, and to file for divorce at the same time. This was six years ago. He asked me about giving up the job. At that time, I could afford to manage all of this relatively easily, so I said, do it. I was very supportive. So he did, and the divorce was straightforward, and he lived here. But he still felt enormously guilty about the children.

They were grown up by this time, weren't they?

Yes, but he still felt guilty. The marriage – in a way, it was a joke. I said, if the 29th of February falls on a Saturday, that's the only day I'd consider marrying you. It was all very lighthearted. But then I looked in the diary, and it was going to be a Saturday. So he said, all right then, we'll get married. I was so shocked!

That was a very happy time. We had a really nice day and a big party. That was his gesture to me, to try and put right all the pain of the previous years. That was the way we both saw it, actually, as a gesture to each other about being secure. Whatever happened, even though the relationship isn't easy, there are still elements of it that are still worth it.

It's still difficult?

Yes, especially the physical side.

Because of his illness?

No, it's me, it's psychological, because of the abuse. I find at times, I just don't like to be touched. I find it difficult to relax. I'm always very wary and very cautious about physical relationships. I think in fact I'm now trying to come to terms with that early part of my life, get it into perspective, why I allowed it to happen or at least left myself wide open to it for so long – perhaps I should have left earlier, I don't know. It would be nice to be able to shelve it totally and think it didn't cause me pain any more.

I would imagine that if you found the right therapist, you could be helped to move on. I had a wonderful counsellor, Charleen – I feel sure that she would be able to help you. But she's in Bristol. You have to find the right person.

It's finding somebody I can trust.

Yes. You have to trust the person you're working with. You told me on the phone that Ted constantly challenges you.

Yes. He challenges my thinking on the world. He often comes at it from a completely different angle. We talk a lot and I really enjoy that, trying to find the truth. Ted challenged me a lot when we first met, what relationships are about. What I do believe is that so long as you're not causing pain to anybody, whatever relationships you have, that's all right.

But Ted was causing pain to you. How was that OK?

He was causing pain, but he didn't acknowledge that the pain was there, and the truth was that it wasn't always there. It was in my weak moments, but at other times I would think, I can be as free as a breeze. But when another man rang me – as soon as I behaved the same as he did – Ted started behaving quite differently towards me. Much more protective.

But he did that to me all the time. He was always talking about other women and his relationship with Pauline. Sometimes it was easy to handle and I wasn't hurt, but the longer the relationship went on, the more I got hurt. I was aware, too, that these were precious years flitting by and I didn't know what would happen in the long term. So I became more resentful, the longer it went on.

Since you've been married, have there been any other women?

No. In fact, in truth, since our relationship began he hasn't had a physical relationship with another woman other than Pauline. All of it was just chat. He's admitted he hasn't wanted anybody else.

He's got a great sense of humour, too. He taught me how to laugh. And even how to smile. He does make me laugh. Sometimes, we're really foolish and stupid, like children. But it's very private. That's part of what keeps the relationship going. The hard thing is not being able to talk about having children. It's like grieving. I would have liked to have known, to do it at least once. But he really doesn't want children.

I think seeing the beauty in life is what it's all about. Trying to comfort yourself with the good things.

CHAPTER 9

ADDICTION

CHRISSIE

I met Chrissie, a warm, attractive young woman with an enviable figure and dreadlocks, in central London. An astonishing variety of jewellery was attached through multiple piercings in her nose, ears, lip and tongue and, she told me, hidden parts of her body. She had told me she was currently living with a difficult man, and that the problem was drug abuse.

Chrissie began by telling me about her previous partner, who died of a drug overdose. I would imagine that many women would think of him as difficult, but Chrissie took his peculiarities in her stride: as far as she was concerned, he was not a difficult man.

My previous partner was a transvestite. We stayed together and I just dealt with it, like you deal with somebody stealing your clothes. It was like living with a sister sometimes! Did you borrow this?

I dunno, maybe it's just the type of person I am, I just didn't think it was much of something I had to deal with. But it wasn't until I saw other people's reactions to it that I thought, wo!, what is this? It was strange, because it wasn't always just the straight people's reaction. It was my gay friends who said, isn't this a problem? And I said no, I had no problem.

He wasn't just a transvestite at home, for sex; it was something he did to go out and things like that. I think the problem I had was, being very bisexual, I couldn't understand why he wasn't as well. He was a transvestite but he was still very, very heterosexual. That was the hardest thing for me to come to terms with and to understand. I had expectations of what this meant; I thought, great, we can deal with this. But it was my expectations of what it meant that caused problems at the beginning, coupled with other people's reactions. The stereotypical assumptions, oh he must be a pervert, child molester type thing.

Let's start from the beginning of that relationship. How did you meet? How did it develop? How old were you?

I was in my late teens. It was the first relationship where I left my home to go live with somebody. We met on the university campus, there was a band playing. I met this person, not realising he was in the band or anything – which is a recurring theme with me, I meet people not realising they're musicians. It wasn't too long afterwards that I found out about the cross-dressing, a couple of months, at most.

Was he trying to hide it from you?

No. It was just something that had never come up, there was no hiding it. I think it just organically grew. I honestly don't think he'd ever cross-dressed before he lived with me. I think that being with me maybe freed him up enough to do this.

I remember the first time he shaved his legs – I was there for all those little firsts. And I remember him getting dressed and saying, 'Is this OK, is this the way you wear things like this?' So it was almost like a sisterly relationship. You'd have to say things tactfully, and sometimes inside I would be dying of laughter and I might crack a smile, but I always made it seem encouraging, never, like, laugh in this person's face.

Because of Chrissie's attitude, something that would disturb many women doesn't worry her at all. In fact, she facilitates her partner's transvestism.

But it wasn't something that his whole life was centred around. I have met some people who would have nothing without their cross-dressing, no sexuality, nothing. It's pretty much what they live for. But with him it was just a small slice of so many other things. He was a brilliant musician, a drug addict, a brilliant artist, we lived at the beach. . . He spoke Russian. . . he was an amazing person. And also his political ideals were very unusual, coming from southern California. . . he was a communist.

He was quite into pornography, and I just found that so boring! We could afford videos, and it was funny because you know, I'd just sit there and say I'm sorry, I'm bored, and reach for a book. It rarely got me in the mood.

But to get back to the cross-dressing. . . I never felt strange going out in public with him. It may have been the place – we were living in Los Angeles – or the types of places we would go to; we wouldn't go to places where people would say, my God, there's a man in a dress, we'd go to fetish clubs and things like that. He wouldn't go completely in women's clothes to the market or something like that, though eventually he was one of these people who always wore women's knickers. I used to tease him, saying it's a comfort thing, isn't it? Knowing darn well that women's knickers are the most uncomfortable things.

Luckily, we had the sort of lifestyle that made it easy. It wasn't as though he would lose his job if people found out. His father was all right; we lived with his father through this whole thing. He was also a very well known musician. He had met a few other people who were also into cross-dressing and they would come over but his dad would not bat an eye – he had no problem with it.

It was just a normal, everyday thing with you – you were living in a different reality from most other people.

Exactly. We used to go down to my parents' house and my mum would say, I hope he doesn't dress like that. . . and she'd give me a situation where people would look at him. It was such a ridiculous thing to say. It was OK with her for him to dress like that going out, but if he started to cross-dress during the day, then I should move out. But to me it didn't make any difference. I don't know, maybe I was young enough that it didn't mean that much to me. Maybe it was because he was so good looking it didn't matter what he wore. You know, a lot of men, if they decided to cross-dress I'd have a problem with it, mostly because of the aesthetics involved. This man was gorgeous. He would look good in anything. [*She stops briefly, wiping tears from her eyes.*] Gosh,

I'm. . . I'm sorry, I'm just starting to think how much I miss him. I do miss him a lot.

His band made it big. They went from playing universities to playing stadiums. I met him about the time their first record hit the top ten. They were opening up for very well known people after that. The transvestite stuff happened before that; it became part of his stage persona. There was nothing cheap about this man; he had enough money to get the best of everything. It wasn't overly girlie, either. What he had underneath would be very, very feminine – I don't know what that means. A lot of people could analyse that but I had no problems as we were getting undressed, finding really nice things. I'd say, ooh, that's nice – so tactile.

It's funny, I've gone from my partner stealing my underwear to a new partner and I steal his underwear! In fact, he has banned me from wearing any of his clothes ever again – because my daughter was wearing his clothes too until he said, that's it, no more.

But there's an anomaly in our culture, isn't there? Women can wear men's clothes but not the other way around.

The Annie Hall look, yes. Our culture doesn't class women dressed as men as sexual deviants.

But your partner wasn't a sexual deviant.

He had no paraphilias at all. Boring though it may sound, he was quite straight when it came to sex. Almost too straight for me. There was nothing kinky about this man at all. It was really funny when we went out at night and we were in a straight establishment, you could almost hear the Christians praying for us!

The drugs. . . I've always been around drugs and I've always done drugs, until recently. Mostly because I'm getting older and I can't recuperate as fast from them. And I think – I mean I know he had been around them and he had experimented with them; but in our relationship I was the one who'd go out once a week or once a month, depending how much money I had, and do a bit of drugs.

I've no idea what triggered the drugs. It didn't bother me. This person made enough money that the drugs were not a problem. It didn't increase my drug-taking any; I'm not an addictive person, I don't know why. I can take or leave them. I don't have to have them – same with food and alcohol.

It was hard towards the end. It was the distance that bothered me. As he got more and more drug addicted. . . We're talking heroin now, he was shooting smack. And after about four months, he could function well at work, but at home, doing drugs and having emotions and being with somebody was too much for him.

How did you deal with this? Did you have rows about it?

No. We never argued. We would talk about it so I understood what was happening. At first I had doubts, I'd ask him if he didn't love me any more, if this was not working. . . But he never tried to hide this from me. What made it easy to stay with him was that we did talk about it. So it wasn't a situation where I felt I had to go. But things did change. It wasn't that I was on my own, but the closeness wasn't there.

I get the impression that heroin would have created significant problems in the relationship if it had continued for longer.

Strangely, the sex was good, though. There was no problem. Heroin gives you a very sexy feeling, what happens with heroin is a man gets an erection and it's there for ever. So that at least was worth staying around for. But we weren't a couple that had sex all the time anyway. The thing that kept us together was that he kept talking to me.

And then he was gone. Dead. Soon after that, I made my way to England.

With a great big hole in your life.

Yes, but I really didn't realise it until a few years later. After his death, I immediately got off with somebody else and got pregnant, had my daughter in Los Angeles, and came over here as soon afterwards as I could. I'd made such a different life for myself. I mean, completely different. I had a baby and moved to a nice little town in Warwickshire. From LA to that.

At that point in my life, I did not want my family around. They were not the people I wanted to turn to for comfort. I did make a conscious effort to be somewhere they could not drive to. That's why I'm here. And it wasn't for a few years, when a friend from LA tracked me down, that it actually hit me that he had gone. This friend wrote me a letter. . . I started reading this letter and it hit me. All that stuff I had never dealt with. I hadn't dealt with any of it. For quite a few years I had nothing to do with men. Nothing. Until my current partner.

Your current man – this one is the difficult man. Your previous one, whatever the outside world and your family thought, wasn't difficult as far as you were concerned.

This one, everybody outside thinks he is perfect. My family, everyone. But he is the slipperiest person I have ever come across. He had his first hit in the music business when he was fifteen and he's in his thirties now; and you do not survive in the music business that long without really developing some bad ways.

The crucial difference between this man and the previous one seems to be that Chrissie feels she cannot trust him.

How long have you been with him?

Just two and a half years. We were from the same group of friends. I had had a relationship with one of the women in the group; that was falling apart and we all went out to a party one night and it just went from there. I don't drink much and he was the only other sober person in the room. I didn't think he was anything like my previous partner, didn't know he was a musician too.

You made a conscious effort not to go for the same type of man? But this one is another musician!

Yes, but I didn't know it! It was a completely different kind of music than I would ever listen to. Techno music. . . don't ask me to name a song! It means nothing to me.

What was funny was my impression of this man.

You showed me his photograph. He looks like a rock star, with his long hair, the whole image.

I thought – he travels a lot, he's obviously got money, he's got connections – he must smuggle drugs. I just thought – that was the only thing I could think of. That, or he was a straight businessman who just hung out at weekends with my friends.

I was seeing this guy for a few weeks, I was quite attached to him, we were really into each other, all the nice stuff you do, and he said, oh, I might have to go away for my work. So I said, 'what is your work?' And he looked at me and said, 'I'm a musician.' And I said, 'Oh, no, shit!' But I was in too far to turn round and walk away at that point. If it had been a week before I'd have turned round and said, no, I'm not doing this musician thing again.

Is there something about musicians that makes them difficult?

Just that I didn't want to deal with a musician again.

You didn't want any echoes of the previous relationship?

Yes, yes, exactly. I wanted to break every pattern going. My previous partner, the one that died, he wasn't the first musician I'd been out with.

Chrissie went to great lengths to avoid reminders of her previous life, not because it was difficult but because it had ended with such grief – grief that she has still not finished working through.

The present one, he came over one day, and I'd been doing some methadone. I box, and I'd been hit in the jaw really badly, and I couldn't talk easily. So he thought maybe it was the painkillers. But the next time he came round, there was a tourniquet on the floor, and he looked at my arms and said, 'Have you been shooting up?' And I said, 'Just once, I don't do it often.' And he really lost it on me. His sister had overdosed when she was fourte, it all just came out. He said, 'If we have this relationship, I don't want you doing it ever again.' So I thought, fair enough, I can live without it, I want to give this relationship a go; I'm expecting things to be different with him, so this is a good way to do it.

That lasted about three months before I started noticing that he was talking in that junkie way, you know, they don't talk fully, kinda nasal. It was little things. I'd notice it out in public. But this whole time, I was saying to him I fancy doing some, sometimes. And he'd say, 'You're a sad woman. Why do you need drugs? That's really disgusting. You can get along without them. I don't like people who need drugs.' Really making me feel bad because once in a while I might fancy getting off my face. Even though it's very clear to people that know me, it really is a recreational thing. Instead of getting drunk, I just like to veg out for a couple of days.

He made me feel really bad about myself, constantly berating me. To the point where I wasn't seeing friends that were involved with it and things like that. Which is very strange for me, because usually I'm quite pig-headed about these things. But I wanted things to be different.

We went up to my parents for Christmas and he was so ill. I didn't get it at the time, but he was detoxing. That was why he was so sick. He hadn't been shooting up, he'd been smoking, so there were no visible traces.

You must have seen this before, surely?

Yes, but I couldn't imagine that could be the explanation. I kept thinking, his eyes look pinned [minute pupils] and red... but no, he was so anti-drugs because his sister had OD'd. I kept thinking there had to be some other explanation. But it just got worse and worse. And our physical relationship was just dying. And I started feeling insecure, thinking he was seeing somebody else, that he didn't love me.

There was also the smell. When people do heroin, you can smell it in the sweat. Like eating garlic. To cover up this smell, he was spraying my really nice perfume around the house. I mean, he was really trying to cover up hard. And finally, we ran into some other friends in a club and they said, wow, what is he on? So I thought, it's not just me.

He had given me every excuse. By this time I was hounding

him, trying to find out what was wrong. He said, 'I went to the doctor and he's really worried because my blood pressure's too high.' And me not being a medical person, I thought maybe you do get pinned when you have high blood pressure. I didn't know – I'd never been around high blood pressure before.

Then this one night, I said, 'What is going on?' And he said, 'I've been taking a lot of Valium, that's why I'm acting this way.' But within fifteen minutes it all came out, that he'd been strung out on heroin for six months and was doing huge amounts, spending lots of money. Again, I had no idea, because this was another man that had a lot of money coming in. With somebody like me, if I got addicted to drugs somebody would know, because I'd always be scrounging for money; but I didn't have that tell-tale sign.

Now, a year or so later, I will not believe a word that comes out of this man's mouth. Which is weird. I couldn't care less if he went off and fucked half the girls on every continent, I don't care. But if he gets strung out on drugs, I don't wanna deal with it. I am the one that has to pick up the pieces when he comes home.

Chrissie is dealing with a variety of issues here. First, the way the man behaves when he is strung out on heroin; second, being reminded of the period leading up to her previous partner's death from heroin; third, her partner's dishonesty; fourth, the double standard by which he forbids her drug use while indulging himself. There is anger, grief and loss of trust, simultaneously.

So what happened then, when you finally knew?

It hit me hard. Like, what? First of all, my partner is a drug addict, heavily, and he's not happy with it. The previous one, it was no problem, he was happy with it.

Except that he died.

Except he died. There is that problem. But I didn't have to deal with somebody who was doing drugs and not happy with it. I think the guilt, and knowing that he had given me such a hard time about drugs, was the reason there was no sex by this time. That hit me really hard. Then I went through the thing, you didn't tell me because you didn't want to share. You are selfish. And I knew he still had some in the house.

But I decided to do everything I could to help him get better. He made it very obvious that he did not want to continue doing that, that was it. Living here in central London, there's about a three and a half months' waiting list to get any help. He did actually go to one of the alternative clinics; I don't know if that helped with the physical stuff but I think it was useful. He also set up some counselling sessions for me, but I wanted to get my own head straight before talking to anyone else. I never went to talk to anybody about his addiction.

After he told me, we got through the weekend without speaking to each other. Because he was still doing it. He still wouldn't give me any – he was still very against me doing it – so I was here in my own house, looking at this man completely off his face, thinking, I hate you for being off your face, I hate you for getting at me for wanting to get off my face – I just couldn't be in the same room with him. I don't know how we got through the weekend. Come Monday, I didn't go to work, I went to the gym and pulled every muscle, working out so hard.

Chrissie is trying to deal with her anger by working out at the gym. She is unable to confront her partner with it, even though he is in her house acting in a way that is unacceptable to her.

When I came home he'd gone down the Portobello Road to this clinic. I just took three weeks and stayed home, and babysat that man.

There were times he was so sick, his whole body was shaking so much, I had to lie on top of him to stop his body, like, seizing. Because I had never gotten into drugs that much, I had never seen anybody be that ill from them. It showed me how much his addiction had progressed. In six months he had got a full addiction. He was spending hundreds of pounds a week buying huge amounts – well, what seemed like huge amounts to me – probably more than I would ever use in my life.

After that, I could not believe a word that man said. I used to be very trusting, I believed people, gave them the benefit of the doubt. But now, anything he says, I try and find an ulterior motive in what he's saying. Or try and figure out if he's telling me the truth. Because he lied to me, blatantly, in my face, for more than six months.

It seems that much that was valuable to Chrissie in this relationship has now been destroyed. Yet she still makes sacrifices in the hope of helping him and salvaging the relationship.

But I did stay home and get him through it. The only time I left him was to take my daughter to school and bring her home. I always made sure that one of his friends was there if I wasn't.

What about your daughter? How did this affect her? Did you worry about that?

No, because we kept it so separate from her. It was as though somebody was going through the flu. She didn't see the really bad times, luckily – those all happened when she wasn't here. She spends time at her friend's house at weekends quite a lot, she'll stay overnight, so nothing changed in her schedule. She was ten years old when this all happened. . .

I'm still with that man, and it's hard, but with everything we've gone through, I don't want to throw it away. After the babysitting, my life didn't get back to normal for a long time. I can't feel as good about my relationship as before because I don't trust the man. And this is a person who goes away a lot due to the industry he works in. When he's here in London, if he's out an extra few hours, I just think, oh–oh. . . I have a feeling he's doing drugs.

He has lapsed a few times, he's gone back to it and lied to my face, but now there's no way I'm gonna believe it because I know.

Now you know that what you see is what's going on. He can't fool you any more.

I knew at the beginning, but I never believed it, because he was in so much denial, I gave him the benefit of the doubt. It sounds stupid, but I had no proof. But now he can't tell me any stories. When he comes off the road and he's been doing drugs, it's very hard to deal with.

What makes it so hard to deal with?

Because he feels so bad about himself, he's not an easy person to have around. You don't just pick up where you left off, you have to get over this first. It would be nice, when he comes home, to be able just to say 'I missed you.' 'I missed you too.' Not 'Oh, this, not again.'

How do you see the future?

I don't think about the future at all. I just deal with it as it happens.

Is there a point at which you'd say, this isn't worth it?

It doesn't really cause me that much pain. It's one of those out of sight, out of mind things.

Chrissie reveals a pattern of coping with distress by distracting herself and ignoring the problems in her life. She had avoided the pain of grieving over her previous partner in a similar way. However, at the same time, she is maintaining her own strength and individuality by engaging effectively with the outside world.

If he's on the road for six weeks, I can get on with my life. I can deal with things and I don't have him here messing up what I'm trying to get accomplished for myself and my daughter. When he comes back, I can tell if he's been doing it. It's not as if he continues to do it when he's here. I just try to deal with things from day to day as they happen, I don't think about the future.

Are you actively trying to keep him straight, or do you feel it's up to him?

I'm more aware of situations and I try to keep him out of them sometimes. But it's not something I'm militant about. If I'm on tour with him I try to steer clear of certain situations, or certain people. But one of his friends that had the babysitting role before I did, we're still quite close with that person.

The amount of money was sickening. For someone like me, who doesn't have a lot, I knew how much money this man had and it was down to not a lot. I was thinking how we could have put that in property – it was that much money. We were in Barbados looking at plots of land. And I just looked at him and said, 'We could buy three plots of land with what you spent.'

But, saying all that, he does have his good points. He does help me out when I need it. He doesn't support me. He pays the phone bill and the house insurance, and most of the expensive things in this flat are his; but I pay my own rent, and when he's not here I buy the groceries. This is my place, my universe; he's like a satellite that docks at intervals. It was more just taking the time out of my life that was a shock. Plus, having trusted him, having it all hit me in the face so hard. And a lot of it was my own, how could you have been so stupid?

The only person I told thought I had been really stupid. But I couldn't share this with people – it could be very damaging to him. Smack is still the big no-no drug. If he was a rock 'n'roll musician he could be out about it, but not techno. This is people that grew up on Ecstasy, they wouldn't touch smack. It does have a huge stigma.

I could have easily gone for counselling, but by the time I got to the point where I could be receptive to it, I didn't need them. The only thing I wanted help with was trusting him, not dealing with his addiction. But the only person who can get me through that is myself.

Does he still lie to you?

No, no, not now. But still I don't trust him. I've not got to the point where I'm going to end this relationship. I think it's the time I get by myself that helps. There will be a time, if things get worse, there will be a time when I'll say forget it, but we're certainly not there now. I'm the kind of person that can take so much, then I'll completely cut the person off. Which is probably not a good way to deal with things but that's the way I am.

I don't have any plans. I'm not saying, if he does it again in two months' time I'm throwing him out, or in two years if he hasn't done it I'm going to marry him – I don't have those sort of goals. I've got more important things to think of, like how I'm going to provide for a teenage daughter. I don't have the energy to waste on how I'm going to live with this man.

CHAPTER 10

PSYCHOLOGICAL PROBLEMS

SOPHIE

I met Sophie in the foyer of the impressive glass and steel office block where she holds down a prestigious job. She stands tall and seems to have considerable confidence. But her manner is warm and caring. She was intrigued by the idea of my book, and offers her story because, although the problems in her relationship are not solved, she feels that she is a survivor.

Having promised anonymity to all the women who contributed to this book, I asked her if she would like to choose the name by which she would be known.

> Call me something nondescript – like Sophie. Sophie's a name that implies wisdom, although as is about to be manifest, there's very little to be had!

These self-deprecating remarks seem out of character. Although they may signify nothing more than nervousness at the start of a very personal interview with a stranger, it is perhaps more likely that they reflect Sophie's lack of confidence in the context of her relationship with her husband. She is in fact far from nondescript – nor does she see herself as such, as her interview makes clear.

> We met six years ago, in September. After a short stay abroad I came back and we started living together in July. We bought a house, which was something he'd never had; he was absolutely delighted with the fact that he was a property owner. We got married eighteen months later, so we've been married three and a half years.

He wanted to marry me the day we met. He introduced himself with, 'Hello, I'm madly in love with you and I want to marry you.' To which I responded, 'Yup, OK, fair enough, if that's what you want!'

That sounds to me like a strange reaction to a very strange opening gambit. Do you tend to go along with what other people want?

Yes, I'm very easygoing and also I've never been bored in my life, so I tend to make my own entertainment. So consequently, if somebody else wants to do something, that's fine by me. I have no problems with that at all.

Even if it's something as important to you as marriage?

Well I was actually joking because I thought he was joking. But when it came down to it I saw him and saw his reaction to me, and that throwaway comment that he made – although in his case it was sincerely meant – about I'm madly in love and I want to marry you – that indicated something to me, that he was devoted enough to want to marry me straight away.

To me it would indicate something quite different – that the man either liked to make grand meaningless gestures, or that he lived in a fantasy world which would be potentially dangerous because it could not allow for the reality of what the woman is. But Sophie, too, was after a fantasy romance.

Because what I've always wanted out of a relationship is a man who has no previous convictions, as it were. I don't ever want a man who has said any of the loving or romantic things to anybody else, I couldn't bear it. I've got to be the first and only one.

I'm not talking about sex. I'm just talking about devotion. Because I couldn't stand the idea of sharing anybody emotionally. Physically, I wouldn't have minded – they could have had every woman in the world – because if they'd had sex without romance, that trivialises the sex anyway, so even the sex wouldn't have been important. But that was something I was always very keen on, finding a man who was emotionally a virgin, if not physically. And in fact Steve was. The other aspect was this total devotion and love - not in a sort of flattering or grovelling, sucking up sort of way, but a genuine devotion. He couldn't take his eyes off me, couldn't take his hands off me, and constantly he would tell me how much he loved and adored me, and I would do the same to him. It was very important to be totally the centre of his universe.

How long did that last?

It lasted until we moved in together. The night we moved in together. That should have been the most romantic night of our lives, because Steve was very excited about the beautiful cottage in the country - it's a lovely house - and we'd moved in together. We didn't have a bed so we pushed some cushions on the floor. And that was the first night he didn't want sex. He became totally uninterested in sex after that. As if he'd got what he wanted, which was a beautiful girlfriend whom other men would envy, a beautiful house that other people would envy, and - again for the first time in a long time - he'd got a car and lots of material things. And he was just delighted to have those material things.

And you brought those things with you? You brought those things into his life?

I made it possible for him. I had no money but we were both working, so we could afford to buy a house together, and he had more self-confidence because he was able to see that people looked at him in a new light. He wasn't just somebody who was a brilliant musician any more. His attitude towards his music was, I'm not a performing animal. I hate performing, I hate playing. People had mostly viewed him as an incredibly talented, if rather strange, person. Whereas now he was being viewed as somebody handsome, urbane, delightful.

A man of substance.

Yes. People wondered how on earth he had managed to get somebody so intelligent and good-looking, because in the past the only people he'd been seen with were - I don't want to sound bitchy - but they were dogs. They were not very bright, they were very, very aggressive, and also very unattractive. And puritanical as well.

It is impossible for me to judge to what degree this is an accurate picture of Steve's ex-girlfriends. Most likely, there is some truth in it. Coupled with the assertion that Steve was a virgin, this choice of girlfriends might have reflected intense guilt about sex and a desire to avoid temptation.

Which is quite interesting because they should have suited him better because he is a puritanical person. But that's not what he wanted. It sounds harsh, but I'm trying to analyse it in the cold light of day.

How old were you?

I was twenty-six when I met him. He's three years older than me, but still the youngest man I've ever been out with.

This isn't the first time you've lived with a man, is it?

Oh no. I've lived with three. The first was thirty-odd years older than I. The reason I lived with him, though I wasn't particularly struck on him, was that I felt rather sorry for him because he had a bit of an unhappy life – he'd moved a long way from home and he was lonely – and also because I couldn't go back and live with my parents and I had to live somewhere. I was just about to go to university, so I moved in with him and spent all the holidays with him.

It seems that Sophie makes a habit of trying to rescue men for whom she feels sorry. She clearly wants to feel needed.

I went out with some people when I was at university, I lived with my fiancé for a year before we broke off the engagement, and in between, when I was in Oxford as a graduate, I lived with one of the dons, who again was about thirty years my senior.

So your husband is very different from all your previous men, just as you are very different from his previous girlfriends.

Totally. Totally. Absolutely. In fact, in many ways I was his choice. I think that's what made him so delighted at first: I was the first woman he had chosen. He had an idea in his mind of what he wanted in a woman: what he wanted her to look like, act like and be like, and when he saw me, it wasn't really as foolish as it appeared, going up to me and saying 'I'm madly in love with you and I want to marry you' because I was the embodiment of all his fantasies about the character and looks and behaviour of the woman of his dreams.

Finding a man who regards you as *the woman of his dreams* is in itself a fantasy situation for many young women, but a man who chooses a specific dream above the range of experience that reality can offer, for such a long period of time when he was sexually mature, must be very anxious about dealing with reality.

Whereas, as I said, women who were attracted to him and who asked him out – and with whom he went out, but only because he had nothing better to do of a Saturday night – were not his choice and so consequently he was marking time until he could find what he really wanted.

It sounds as though he ceased to value you as soon as he'd got you.

That's very much how I felt. I felt almost as if he viewed me as yet another possession and not as a person in my own right.

Fantasies are not people in their own right. They are the property of the individual who creates them.

Though he was full of admiration for me as a character. I'm university educated, he isn't, but you wouldn't be able to tell to talk to him, he's a very naturally intelligent person. But he hated school and was such a loner and so – neurotic, I suppose – he left school early, didn't get any qualifications.

Once again, Sophie is nurturing a damaged individual. Clearly this must bring her some satisfaction, but at a heavy cost.

The major problem is the physical one, not an intellectual one. We had – we still have, now – a wonderful relationship as far as talking is concerned. We chat, we laugh at the same things, we have a great sense of humour. And we have lots of – you know, like couples do, they have their own cute cuddly little ways. But as far as anything more than fraternal affection is concerned, he's just not interested and basically, wasn't, from that night. And you can imagine how, on what should have been the most romantic night of our lives, the first time we'd moved in together as a couple, he wasn't interested in me and hasn't been significantly so since.

Did you think that things would change when you married? It had been like this for well over a year, and you still married.

It was because we were planning to get married all the time. I had a showdown with him and the reason for the showdown was because I had come across – I wasn't prying, I never did pry, but now I pry all the time – the itemised telephone bill from his work. And I realised that all the days he had spent away from me, he had been telephoning 0898 numbers. Almost simultaneously, I discovered that he had started buying pornography. Now I know he's always bought it – his mother told me he always had – but for the first year of our relationship I never saw any evidence of it. No reason to suspect he was doing anything other than having a normal relationship with me. But during that first summer, when we were living together, I discovered that what he was doing was waiting till I got up in the morning, then when I'd gone out of the room, he was. . . he was not interested in sex with another person, he just wanted to do it by himself.

He feels safer with fantasy women? You were his fantasy – maybe you turned out too real. Maybe reality is more demanding or less exciting than fantasy.

That might be it. Interestingly, I know that men are supposed to be very visual, I know that men buy these magazines for the pictures. If I go through Steve's hidden stash of dirty magazines, they don't fall open at the pictures, they fall open at the stories. It's supposed to be women who are turned on by words and men who are turned on by the visual images. But he never even looks at those women. He doesn't buy it for the pictures.

So he likes to imagine his fantasy objects, whereas you're real.

That's the problem. I don't mind being a sexual fantasy object – I have always worn stockings, I've always liked nice underwear, I like a bit of leather. . . I'm not kinky, I just like that sort of thing, I think it's elegant. And I know some men would absolutely kill for that. Steve did at first, he thought it was fantastic. He used to say, 'I've never seen a woman who has such beautiful under-wear', and literally, he did, he used to masturbate in the morn-ing when he could see me getting dressed. Now, that I didn't mind – there's nothing wrong with masturbation at all – not when you're the figure of their desire. That's very flattering. It's normal. But the lines are blurred between what is normal and acceptable and what isn't. I'm not madly adventurous by nature, but whatever is making the other person happy at that time, I will join in wholeheartedly.

Steve's mother has a lot of very peculiar views about sex. She was abused as a child by her stepfather and consequently she instilled a lot of very puritanical, neurotic attitudes in Steve. When she was a child, her stepfather used to insist that she and her sister should never lock the bathroom door. So now the bathroom is totally sacrosanct. You never let anybody in there. Anything you do there is totally and utterly private. Now I'm not a pervert, I don't want to watch Steve about his ablutions, but one of the first things that I noticed that was odd about him was the way he would always lock himself in, whether he was having a bath or whatever he was doing, and he would not let me in. It's not as if we have lodgers or anybody else who might walk in on him. He wouldn't ever take a bath with me, even though that was one of his earliest fantasies. We both agreed it would be so romantic to have a bath together. But it never materialised.

Because it was wonderful in fantasy but the reality is frightening. He must recognise that he has a problem.

He refuses to discuss it. This is part of the problem. I'm very ver-bal, I'll talk about anything to anyone – that's why I'm talking to you now! I have no embarassment about anything. As far as I'm concerned, we're all human and we all have the same bodies, we have the same bodily functions, and we have similar mentalities. Basically, we're bound together by similarity. Whereas Steve has a very different, very puritanical attitude. He won't discuss things. That's a major problem for me. Every time I try to talk about this, he will say, 'I don't know what you're talking about', or 'I don't know what you mean', or 'What problem?'

It doesn't matter how I raise the issue. I've been tearful, I've been angry, I've been upset, I've been calm, I've been reasonable. It makes no difference. Always I get one of those phrases for putting me off discussing things with him.

But it is a problem for you. How does he react when you tell him you've got a problem with it?

Well, normally I do put it in that way, because I didn't want to say, 'you're peculiar', I wanted to say 'I'm hurt, because you think more of these books than you do of me.' I'm not puritanical in any way, shape or form; if he wants to read dirty books that's fine, so long as he has a healthy sex life with me. The fact that he's choosing this trash over me is a blow to my self-esteem which is almost too much to bear.

I used to say 'I'm trying to resolve this, what's the matter with me?' And I got to the point where I was so depressed, if I were walking down the street and a bus were to run me over, it wouldn't have bothered me. I haven't actually been suicidal – I wouldn't have deliberately stepped in front of it – but I didn't care if I lived or died. But he didn't understand.

Steve wouldn't understand. Sophie's desire for a relationship that has full existence in reality is something he has not experienced. Because of his upbringing, he has become too afraid of committed sexual relationships. I wonder if in fact Steve was sexually abused as a child.

He's always been a person who would cry easily, he's very, very emotional, and that was one of the things that attracted me to him, the fact that he would confide very personal things, all the things that really hurt him, he could talk about to me. And it was almost as if he'd got over a lifetime of never having a friend in whom he could confide when he met me. And then I'd served my purpose. That was it. He'd had one fantastic relationship with one attractive woman, he'd had one friend in whom he could confide. He'd done that, he'd had that, so now he could throw it away.

But you still talk about other sorts of things. A lot of that friendship is still there.

Oh yes, we still do get on. And I do love him still. Partly, that's because I remember the good times, when our relationship was so fantastic, and I know he's capable of that.

Just as fear outlasts experience of abuse, the memory of passion outlasts the reality of it, binding women to men with whom their relationship has deteriorated.

But there are other problems, as well as sex. The major one is his uncontrollable temper. He is the worst example of road rage. I've tried to stop him – because of course he's leaning across me in the passenger seat, gesticulating at other drivers (who have made the most minor and trivial infringement of the rules of the road, but he *has* to tell them) and I'm putting my hands up, saying, 'Don't, Steve, don't do that to them, because one of these days you're going to be gesticulating at somebody who's bigger and stronger and even angrier than you, and then they're going to come after you and rough you up. So it's not a good idea. Just keep calm. You're not going to teach them how to drive, so don't worry about it.' But he will not stop. And the last time, he got so angry that I stopped him. He said, 'You're supposed to be seen to be on my side, you're supposed to back me up.'

Again, Steve does not want Sophie to act as an independent individual. He gets angry when she steps outside the boundaries of what his fantasy woman would do.

Yet he loves my family, he loves them more than his own. Because my family don't judge anybody, they love everybody. They're warm and friendly. But he would say monstrously insulting things to them.

How does that make you feel?

I used to laugh. Couldn't believe he was serious. I'm not the sort of person to get wound up and angry over things easily.

It is unfortunate that Sophie rarely recognises how serious Steve is. She keeps assuming that his reactions will be similar to those she has met among her family and friends. But Steve is not the same; he is a seriously damaged individual.

Also, when we've had minor disasters – a great plumbing disaster in 1993 when mains pressure water shot out all over the house, causing a flood – Steve panicked totally. Which is fair enough because it's a horrible thing to happen. But when I said, it's all right, I'll go next door, I'll call an emergency plumber, I'll call the people who used to live in the house before us, who very conveniently boarded over the stopcock, to tell us where it is and how to sort it – don't worry, I'll do it. Anyway, I went next door because we had no telephone and did that. And when I came back, he was so angry with me. He said, 'You're so smug.' That's one of his major things, if I get angry and shout back at him, which I usually don't because I can't see anything worth getting angry about. The reason he's getting angry is so trivial, it's funny. I'm not demeaning him, not laughing at him, just saying don't worry about it.

You don't take the problem as seriously as he does. Do you think he really wants you to take it seriously?

On occasions I have; I regard it as an over-reaction now. When I found he was hoarding the pornography, for example, I picked up the centre page with the naked woman, tore it in half, stuck a Post-It over the top saying 'If this is what you want, get her in to live with you', left it on our pillow and went out. And then didn't come back for a long time. When I did come back, I found him stuffing pills into his mouth. Not enough to kill himself.

The timing of this parasuicide makes it obvious that its main intention is to frighten Sophie and prevent her from putting pressure on Steve. This does not mean that Steve is not at risk of suicide; such gestures are in fact more common among people who do end up taking their own lives. But Sophie must realise that this is not her responsibility: it really is *his* problem. The most effective strategy for preventing this sort of thing is likely to be to pay no attention to it, and to make it clear that she refuses to be blackmailed.

He's only had two friends, apart from me, in his entire life. One was a young man whom he viewed as an older brother figure. He ended up committing suicide because of marital problems. His other friend was the person who introduced us; she was a middle-aged woman, a very close friend of mine, who was a sort of drinking companion. They used to meet in the pub and chat, and I think he confided quite a lot in her. She was very unstable and she committed suicide as well. So it's worrying. Steve has always been a suicidal, depressive sort of person.

Does that affect you?

If I leave him, he'll kill himself. That's what I worry about. I just can't get rid of him. But he says things that he doesn't back up with actions. Like he says, 'Everything I do, it's all for you. You're the only thing that is in any way a joy in my life.' But if I were a joy, he wouldn't treat me like crap.

I know exactly what you mean. I've often wondered how someone who professes to love me could treat me so badly.

It's horrendous, isn't it? There was I, thinking I was the only person who felt like that. But I suspect it's quite common. And people are beginning to talk about it. In times gone by, you used to hear the usual rant from men: my wife wasn't interested in sex so I had to look for it elsewhere. That's the view that women are respectable, they have the headache, whereas the men are always after it. Whereas nowadays people are beginning to recognise that it's happening more and more the other way around. At first I didn't realise that, I thought there was something wrong with me. I used to get out of the bath and look in the looking-glass and think, where is the ugliness? What is so despicable and foul in me, that he cannot bring himself to touch me?

Now he just ignores me and I've learnt to expect that. But at first, he literally used to push me away if I tried to hug him or touch him in any intimate way. Which you can imagine was extremely hurtful. I no longer do that because I realise that even though my husband rejects me at home, every other man in the street looks at me, or whistles. But I'm ludicrously faithful. If I thought a man even had a girlfriend, let alone a wife, no matter how delightful he was, I couldn't view him as a prospective partner. Similarly, the fact that I'm married means that I will not stray from the path. At the same time, a lot of people whose opinions I value say, well that's not fair, because you haven't got a marriage.

You haven't had sex for years, then?

Well we have, just incredibly infrequently, only when he decides that's what he wants.

He does occasionally want it?

Yes. The problem is that because I never know, because I daren't initiate anything any more because I'm too hurt when he shoves me away, I'm never expecting anything. So I don't enjoy it even when it happens. So I think, well if you're not enjoying it, forget it. Which is such an about-face from how we were at first. For almost a year, it was wonderful.

So you know the possibility is there, within him.

Absolutely. You mentioned about why I married him. It's because I live off how things used to be. That's all that's kept us together, that I remember very clearly how it used to be at first. There was so much honesty in the first ten months of our relationship, intimacy of every kind, there's no way that could have been a fake.

That's a real side of him that you know exists.

I know it does and I sometimes still hope to get that back. But realistically, we've had so many arguments or discussions about it. I say, look, this isn't making me happy. I know you want to have sex every day. If you didn't want sex every day, you wouldn't make sure I was shoved out of bed and into the bathroom while you did what I know you're up to. So for goodness' sake, don't try to pretend you've lost your sex drive, because you haven't. He does it twice a day, I think. So it's not that he doesn't want it, it's just that he doesn't want it with me.

Another of his favourite phrases is, 'Oh well I'm just not virile enough for you.' He tries to throw it back at me, as though I were making an unreasonable demand, or I were some sort of harlot or nymphomaniac. Simply because I'm normal. But I now know it's not me that's abnormal. It's him. I never say that to him, but I know that. So I feel better. I'm no longer tearing myself apart, wondering if there's something wrong with me.

So the way you've learnt to deal with this is by saying, basically I am OK, but he's not.

Precisely. As the Bible says, I looked for the beam in my own eye first, and found that there wasn't one. But there was one in his. I did look within myself before I looked at him. It stands to reason anyway. Everybody who knows me can just tell, I'm a normal affectionate person. The idea that someone who is so affectionate should be kept at arm's length by the one person whom they chose, it's so hurtful. . .

Because of your religious beliefs, do you feel you have to accept this for the rest of your life? You don't believe in divorce, so do you have to accept this marriage?

There is that part of my mind. I was brought up as a devout Roman Catholic, and that is a strong reason for me. I do also believe it, I've never doubted the existence of God. Faith is a gift.

And that belief includes a certain set of rules about how you live your life.

Yes. I don't want to seem hypocritical, but I do think that those rules are there to help rather than hinder you. I do think a marriage is sacred and it's something you should try to keep together to the best of your ability, but I have done that. I don't think that God intends people to suffer in this way all the time. I think these rules are the best way to live your life, but you can't blame people for not being saints. So I don't let my religious beliefs trouble me over-much in this issue.

I can see that there may be little you can do to influence his behaviour in relation to sex. But what about the anger and the rage? How does that affect you?

It makes me tense all the time. I have a very stressful job, you constantly have to think ahead, think on your feet. And you develop physical problems like tension in the neck. I want to be able to go home and relax and have somebody there who isn't trying to trip me up and who isn't demanding, demanding, demanding all the time.

This side of Steve is linked with his immature behaviour in other aspects of life. He avoids taking responsibility for himself, his fate and his actions.

He works near me and we drive to town and back together. And all the way home, in the car, when I should be unwinding and talking to my husband and snuggling up to him, but all I do is sit there totally wound up because of his road-rage anger and his unreasonable comments. There's no charity in him. No charity at all. He says the most awful things about people. His view is that everybody is out to get you, everybody is trying to trip you up.

If he stalls the car he will go into a paroxysm of fear and rage and humiliation. He talks about it: 'Everyone will be laughing at us because we've got a car that doesn't work.' The car figures very prominently in our lives.

Anyway, because he feels everybody's out to get him, he's got to get the boot in first.

Do you think he sees you as a threat too? You are successful and intelligent – maybe he feels inferior?

But he's intelligent too. He has the most phenomenal talent. He was a child prodigy. He is possibly one of the best musicians in the country but he has no sense of self-worth, because he's never worked for it. It's sheer talent. But he doesn't value it. I think that phenomenal talent easily matches my relatively humble, normal talent for what I do. We're different types of people so I'll often get bigger accolades for what I do. If we're in a room, people will look at me. . .

I'm warmer, that's the difference. He is very witty, very intelligent, but I talk to people because I genuinely like them. With Steve, he'll make very witty, amusing comments and people will be taken by them, but there's no warmth. He's not giving, he's throwing things at them.

So people don't give back to him.

Not really, no. And he's never had any friends. I don't think people are out to get him, because I don't think most people think in that way. But possibly it's a measure of his view of others, that he thinks they're laughing at him.

This seems to be more a male thing.

I very much agree with that. And also, it's a class thing. In this country, this is something we are very wary of articulating. Financially, I'm lower class, but the job I do makes me middle class and my family are upper class. I've been brought up to believe that if you love and serve everybody, and have a sense of their worth, then people will give the same back to you. And I've been brought up with the attitude that you are nobody's inferior – not that you're superior either. Steve was brought up with the lower-middle-class attitude that everybody is his superior or wants to be, so consequently he has to spurn people, he has to put them down, he has to be snobbish about people and look down his nose at them in order to appear greater than them.

Your life with Steve seems to be proving that the things you believe about people are untrue! You give, but he doesn't respond by giving back to you.

Precisely. This is why it's so hurtful that the one person in my life who should do that freely is not doing it.

Yet he would be devastated if you went.

So he says.

You don't entirely believe that.

Not entirely. I believe it as far as how he used to be with me; there must have been some profound love at some time. I also believe he would be devastated because he'd be incredibly lonely. But the bit I don't believe is if you love someone so much that if they were to leave you your life would be in ruins, then why would you treat them in that way? Why would you shove them out of the door then call for them to come back?

I can't explain it, but I've had that experience to some degree as well. When I wrote about violence in my Cosmo piece, I wrote that when Colin was depressed he really did treat me worse than the dog, and yet I don't think he would survive it if I left. He's dependent on me. But I think he resents that.

Yes. Steve is the same. There is a dependency, there is an acknowledgement that you're the strong one. At the same time, because Steve has familial and societal pressure on him to be the strong one, and cares about that pressure – I don't give a damn about what people think about me, as long as they don't think I'm an evil person – but he does care about that sort of thing. He feels that he has to be seen to be the boss. Although the comments he makes are totally anti that way of thinking. For example, he has always said he couldn't wait for me to get on and start earning more money so we could settle down and have a family, and he would bring up the children.

Again, Steve seeks to evade responsibility. He wants Sophie to provide him with a family, and with the financial means to support it.

And that was his idea. I was horrified. One, because I like the idea of being a housewife; and two, given what I know about his views about life, the universe and everything, I would dread my children being brought up like that, always looking over their shoulders to worry about what somebody's thinking about them or whether they're doing the right thing. I'd hate them to worry about stepping out of line, about some petty bit of bourgeois etiquette.

He's very dominated by fear, but you're not.

I have no fear of anything! That's a good analysis, I think.

I've found that most people to whom I've gone for advice have listened and said, oh that's terrible, how can you bear that, you poor thing, and questioned me from the thread to the needle about how the relationship has turned out this way. But nobody knows why. Whatever they think, I've got there before them. I've been thinking about this for a long time. And really, there's nothing that could have prepared me for this. Also, there's pride. As I get older, I feel one should have a lot of self-worth. I have a lot of self-worth. The whole thing about looking for it in yourself – I should have known from the start that there was nothing wrong with me. If there was something wrong with me, why is it that every other man I've met. . . I've never, ever seen anything like this in my life before. And I've been out with different types of men, some of whom had low self-esteem, some of whom were arrogant, some of whom were – oh, all sorts of very peculiar people. And normal, well-balanced ones as well. And I've never had a second's difficulty. The only problem was that I didn't want any reminder that they'd ever been out with anybody before – and I recognise that's unreasonable but I don't care!

I wonder if you were setting yourself up to find a difficult man, because of that precondition?

You are absolutely right. Because if you look at the way teenage boys behave, usually they get to about fourteen and they fall madly in love. Then they get a little bit older and it's anything for a quick lay. And it's quite interesting that because Steve has never been through that stage, he's never ever been besotted with anybody before me, he went through it with me and he's going through the, 'Oh I don't care, women are just good for one thing and I'm not even bothered about that' stage with me as well.

So you hope he might grow out of that.

That's what I hope, though I don't know if I'm going to be able to wait around that long. Because I do not relish the idea of bringing children into the world with a man whom I may end up having to leave. I don't want to do that. All my family are the results of broken marriages.

But your own parents have a long and happy marriage.

Yes, I grew up with a good model. Steve's parents, of course, are divorced. His mother was twice divorced.
    I often wonder if he's quite sane.
    The only time I threw a fit was after I found out about his obsession with pornography, and that's the only time I've ever insulted him. I'd been so hurt but I hadn't said anything and he dared to berate me for something or other. I just came out with, 'How dare you talk to me like that, you filthy little pervert!' And that's the only time I have ever insulted him. I've always been so careful not to.

You've been behaving in a very consistent way throughout all this, but things have been tending to get worse. Have you thought of changing? If you got mad at him, how would he react?

I have tried it on occasion. We don't normally argue, because normally I just deadbat all his fuming.

But you're taking it all in!

Yes, I know that. That's why my neck is so painful, I can't turn my head. It all goes to my body and my neck is my weak point.

Sophie sees herself as strong and able to take whatever Steve throws at her. She also recognises that she is not responsible for his behaviour. Nevertheless, she is suffering. Living with this man causes her real pain. She is unable to change the way he acts. He is so deeply damaged that he needs professional help. I doubt that he will ever be capable of behaving in a mature fashion within marriage.

On the occasions when I have fought back and told him what I think of him, and said 'Look, can't you see that this is no way to carry on' – being relatively reasonable but giving him harsh words – he's stormed out of the house and I haven't seen him for hours. Then he's come back as if nothing had happened and there's no need to talk about anything. So it seems futile.

At one point I was keeping a diary, basically letting my thoughts out, writing it all down in a little diary which I kept hidden in a drawer. And everything I've told you – sometimes the pages were marked with tears because I was crying so hard – but you know, if you talk to yourself, you think you're mad so you write it down instead.

It can also help to clarify things.

It does. So I've scribbled down things which contained every ounce of the pain and anguish that he'd caused me, and nobody who read it could be in any doubt as to what was going through my mind. And when things were slightly better, just before we got married, I did say, one of the times we were discussing things, that when I was very depressed and upset about this, I wrote everything I felt down in a diary. I said I wasn't going to show it, but if he'd ever seen it, he wouldn't have treated me that way. He said, 'Oh, that? I read that ages ago.' And I thought, well, he could pretend, and he wouldn't listen, but he'd read all that, he knew what he'd put me through, and he didn't stop doing it.

Are you sure he had read it?

I know he read it. Every word.

So how can he love you?

Well he hates me, I think, sometimes. I think he doesn't know what he wants. He hates himself to the point that someone who loves him like me must also be hateful: if you love me, you must be as awful as I am. I hate to think that there are people who are as screwed up as that.

I'm just glad I'm not a weaker person than I am. Because it's the sort of rejection that nobody – even people who are plain, homely, not much personality, nothing going for them, not very bright – even somebody like that, that you could expect might be treated that way – because it is rotten out there and it's a shallow society and you do get rewarded for being good-looking and you do get rewarded for being intelligent and bright – but nobody deserves that. But you can imagine how much worse it is if you do have a sense of *amour propre*, if you do have a sense of self-worth, you know that someone has no reason to treat you that way, and yet does. You wonder if it's all to do with, there is no honour to be gained by destroying somebody who is weak. Somebody who is strong, if you can destroy them and make them feel like nothing, you've really achieved something. You must be quite good after all. And maybe that's it.

Everybody who knows me says, get rid of him! Send him down the road!

You can't carry on like this.

It's also stopping me having relationships with other people. There's somebody at work I find incredibly attractive. Now, with my marriage almost in ruins, I am starting to look at other people. But I couldn't live with adultery. I could cope with being divorced. I could even cope with being separated. He's broken his side of the contract. My biggest regret of all was actually getting married. If we weren't married, I'd be able to leave him. It's a very awkward situation and I don't know how to get out of it. I just can't get rid of him. If only we could talk – I can't feel happy without true answers. Even if they aren't what I want to hear.

A year after this interview, Sophie was still living with Steve and their relationship was basically unchanged. She said she had come to terms with the situation and that she still loved him.

PART FOUR

SHARED LESSONS

CHAPTER 11

INDIVIDUATION

Creating a mutually satisfying relationship with a difficult man requires decisive steps. Although there are some signposts, each woman has to find her unique route. But until you can see the direction you want to take, you are not likely to make much progress.

The first challenge is to discover and develop yourself. This means getting in touch with your own aims, priorities, values, needs and desires, and learning to trust them. Women's views inevitably differ from their partners'. Yet often, we subordinate our own views to those of other people around us, losing that crucial sense of personal identity. You cannot act effectively in your own interest until you have regained that crucial sense of self.

This is not as straightforward as it might seem at first sight. Many women do not, and indeed cannot, consider themselves in isolation. It may be that we have an inbuilt need to merge, at least to some degree, with the social group to which we belong – which may be as small as the couple. And many of us are carers with responsibilities. So acting in our own interests, as individuals, can be a matter of delicate moral judgement. Nevertheless, I believe that developing that sense of individuation is absolutely fundamental to managing relationships with difficult men. It was an issue that came up again and again, in a variety of forms, in the experiences of the women.

Every mother I spoke to regarded the welfare of her children as paramount. Keeping the home intact for the children is a very strong incentive for staying with a difficult man. It is also a powerful reason for finding a way of managing the relationship that makes it less destructive. No mother wants her son to grow into an abusive man, or her daughter to be vulnerable to abuse.

Vicky put this point particularly clearly when she said, 'I don't want them to see him treat me that way because I don't want [my children] to grow up behaving like that. I don't want my son to grow up like that. . . and I don't want [my daughter] to think this is the way that women are.'

But it is not enough to live for the children alone. To handle difficult men effectively, women have to be clear that they are living for themselves. This, ultimately, benefits the whole family, as Vicky also recognised: 'When he was like he used to be, I only used to think about how he felt, and I used to ignore my own feelings. That was part of the problem. But now, I think of him, but I also think of myself and the children. I always think, if I'm happy then I can be a good mum to the children, which makes them happy.'

Getting in touch with her own feelings and desires was not easy at first; Vicky was totally unaccustomed to trusting herself and she had difficulty making decisions. 'Everything used to be him, all the time,' she explained. 'I never thought how I really thought about things.' And again: 'I hadn't actually thought about what I wanted – it was forever what he wanted. My friends were his friends' wives. I lived in his world.'

Her husband had actively tried to prevent her from thinking for herself: 'He'd say, oh no, no, you have to think how I do. You don't have opinions of your own.' Eventually she lost confidence totally in her own ability to think, make decisions, or cope without him: 'I wanted him to rule my life. I was letting him choose everything for me. He'd broken me. What self-esteem I'd had, I'd lost. I wanted to be told where to go and when to go. I knew I was doing the wrong thing.'

It took a period of enforced separation, followed by counselling, for Vicky to recover her sense of self.

Tessa, too, was living in the shadow of her difficult man. Jolted by a friend's cutting remark, she recalls, 'I really thought, then, gosh, I don't have a life of my own, I'm just the cook. . . I need to do something that's for me.' That decision was the turning point.

For Amanda, who is still struggling to find a way to manage her relationship, problems with individuation block her progress. She does not trust her feelings and finds her own deeply held views unacceptable: 'I still find it bloody difficult, I still sink back into conventional thinking and wish it wasn't happening. . . In theory I can see that love is OK. I can't see any reason to stop somebody loving somebody else. Because I can't see any logical reason why not. Except I feel threatened by it. Because it's what we are desperately trying to teach our children: to love each other. And there's me saying "I don't want you to love her." I can't logically give a reason why not.'

She fails to acknowledge that since feelings are not logical, to expect to apply logic is itself unreasonable. Feelings are important in themselves and should not be overruled because they do not appear to be logical. Love is not logical either – but Amanda seems to test only her feelings, not Chris's desires, against this criterion.

The way she answers questions shows that she believes her husband's view of the situation is more valid than her own: 'I could make it that way, but that would come from me and not from him.' Unlike her, he has confidence in his opinions – which she resents because it contributes to his power within the relationship: 'He is difficult too, a know-it-all man.'

Many difficult men actively seek to control their partners by telling them what they should feel or undermining their self-confidence in a range of ways. This is what appears to be happening in this case. As a result, Amanda would rather believe her feelings are the problem than her husband's behaviour. In addition, she has difficulty acknowledging that what she wants can be legitimate if it is not what he also wants: 'I get confused about my needs. And he's very clear on his needs. He keeps asking what my needs are, but I'm very foggy on them. When I come to think of it, my needs are that he should do this and he should do that, and I can see that that's not the way. I just don't know what to do about it.'

Her husband maintains control over the situation by cleverly twisting her perception of reality. But if Amanda did learn to respect herself enough to value her own feelings, the chimera of harmony in the household would probably vanish.

A man's determination to prevent his wife from learning to manage the situation can be the greatest hindrance to her progress. Those men who perceive change as operating against their interests will tend to put blocks in their wives' way. But a determined woman will win through, as Louise found when she insisted on taking a job. 'All of this I did in the face of utter opposition from Adam. He said I was wasting my time, working with people nobody could respect: what did I think I was doing? I was being Joan of Arc. . . He tore it down all the time. . . Adam has only accepted. . . my job because he realised that if I didn't have that way out, stepping sideways, I would have gone completely.'

Going out to work, or following a significant interest which was not shared with the man, was very important for most of the women. It allowed them to build a life where they could be free from his influence, to develop self-confidence in his absence, and provided an opportunity to mix with people who would support them.

Amanda's experience illustrates the sort of problem that can arise when women do not insist on a separate life. 'Chris went away for eight weeks. But he was just in the next village and continued to come to see me – in fact, perhaps we saw too much of each other, because I was quite enjoying being on my own! We've always been under each other's feet, neither of us has ever gone out to work since we've been living together.'

Here is Vicky's voice again: 'I work with a load of women and it's brilliant. But if Matthew had his way he'd have stopped me going. He made it really awkward for me. . . One day I thought I just wouldn't bother any more, and I said to the women I don't think I'll be coming any more, but they wouldn't have it. They said "Don't you dare, you get here no matter what!" I've been there three and a half years now, and I know now I'd have been so silly if I'd let him get away with that. I didn't let him. I put my foot down. And it's paid dividends. I'm still there, and I still love it, and to be able to speak to women is so important.'

Tessa said of her training, 'I think it's helped me a lot. I opened up tremendously. Looking back, I think Frank's been quite threatened by that, actually. Because it's like he's seen me developing myself in a completely different way. . . As soon as I started my training, it gave me a glimpse of something I really wanted to do, possibly for the rest of my life, so it was really important to me. . . [It was] such a relief, unbelievable, to be with a group of people who accepted me as a fellow human being.'

Tessa, Vicky and Louise were able to step away from their role as their husband's satellite to find their individual direction. For Chrissie and Marian, jobs outside the home offered stability and a sense that they had control over their own lives.

If you have difficulty identifying your personal desires and feelings, it may be helpful to make a list of things that are important to you. These can be big things or little things or a mixture of both. Do this on your own, when nobody is around to distract you. Don't discuss your list with anyone else until you've finished it and thought hard about it on your own. Make sure that these are *your* priorities, not your partner's, nor the priorities you may think you ought to have. Study your list and decide on the order of importance of the items on it.

Then consider how well your life reflects your list. Can you see any way that you might improve the match? Are there things that really matter to you that you are ignoring? Changing your life to match your desires is likely to be a long process, but the first step is to work out what you want. Only then can you set out to get it.

CHAPTER 12

YOUR STRENGTH, YOUR VALUES

Sometimes we lose touch with our own inner strength. Living with a difficult man can make women feel they have little value and no power. Seeing through such illusions is crucial to being in control of your destiny and making your own decisions.

Some men maintain power over women by undermining their self-confidence. Louise's husband told her she was undesirable and that he no longer wanted her. Sophie's husband calls her 'smug' when she copes with disasters instead of panicking, as he does. Colin used to tell me I was stupid and incompetent; my previous husband told me I was fat and unattractive. In both relationships, I went through a period when I had very little self-confidence.

Another way men may seek to control women is by treating them like children. If the woman lacks confidence, she will accept this – as though she were a child and as though children deserve such treatment. Vicky explained how before she changed the relationship, 'if I displeased him, he'd treat me like a naughty child and say, "Right, that's it, I'm going out for the night," and he'd maybe not speak to me for three or four days.'

I, too, was bullied, as I had been when I was a child. On one occasion, when I was becoming aware of what was going on, I wrote down what was said:

Me: I want to help.
Him: Well you can't, can you. Piss off. You're just the stupid child in the corner who never initiates anything.

I crept away feeling useless, as he apparently intended, but angry enough to record the exchange. Eventually, I learnt not to try to help unless I knew exactly what I was offering.

In Amanda's case, the undermining is more subtle: 'He says

he loves me more, now, but I find that hard to accept. I still feel challenged and threatened and competitive.' Very few women would believe that Chris's adamant refusal to give up his 'friendship' with his mistress could possibly reflect the love that he professes to feel for his wife. Similarly, his insistence that he and the other women are not lovers, when they have a sexual relationship, is a distortion that is bound to throw Amanda off balance – for as long as she continues to believe him.

Vicky, in her wonderfully clear-sighted way, tells how things change when a woman gets in touch with her inner strength: 'How I've changed, is I'll say, look, I'm doing this. Are you going to be awkward? Because I'll still do it, I'll find some other way of doing it.' She no longer assumes that her husband is in the right every time they disagree, nor is she willing to pretend to go along with his views. She has come out as an individual who thinks for herself.

Vicky said, 'I put my foot down', when she decided that her husband must change the way he behaved. This was something she had never done before, but she succeeds by sticking firmly to her chosen course of action.

This determination is crucial. Any woman can decide to act in a focused, determined manner. What is required is that we make decisions, identifying our own priorities and values, because these are an essential part of what we are. Then we have to stick to our chosen course of action even in the face of opposition. We decide that what we believe we must do, we will do. This is what I mean by strength.

Stella knows that she is a strong woman. In the early years of the relationship, she says 'I liked seeing myself as the weaker partner' – she was taking what she saw as the feminine role. But in fact, as she later recognised, she was not weak at all; she had power and she used it, sometimes quite cynically: 'I think I found it really amazing that I could have that effect on some-one, that just by saying a few words, he could go absolutely apeshit. It's amazing to have that control, that power.' The crucial change for her was to recognise that she should not use her power destructively, manipulating a very committed man so that she could prove how important she was to him. She needed simply to believe he loved her totally, and not require further proof.

For those of us who, like Vicky in the early years, do not realise that we have access to power within the relationship, the transformation may require a catalyst. For her, a period of separation, when she discovered that she could manage her life far better than she had ever believed, was crucial. Separation continues to be crucial to Louise, who has not yet discovered how to control her husband's abusive behaviour.

When a woman cannot reshape the relationship so that it fits her needs, inner strength is essential to her personal survival in an unsatisfactory situation. Sophie is able to remain married to a man who prefers masturbation to sex because she is in touch with her strong core; she is confident that she is a normal woman: 'He tries to throw it back at me, as though I were making an unreasonable demand, or as if I were a harlot or nymphomaniac. Simply because I'm normal. But I now know it's not me that's abnormal. It's him. I never say that to him, but I know that. So I feel better. I'm no longer tearing myself apart, wondering if there's something wrong with me.'

Nurturing yourself helps you to get in touch with that inner strength. This means different things to different people: it might be anything from relaxing in a hot scented bath to going horse-riding. The crucial thing is that you feel stronger and better after doing it.

For me, gardening is very important; contact with the soil and growing things keeps my core intact. Painting is important in a similar way to Louise.

Assertiveness courses can help to build inner strength, as can psychotherapy and counselling. Sometimes the catalyst for change is insight gained by such means as these. This is a theme to which I shall return in the last chapter of this section.

CHAPTER 13

NEW PERSPECTIVES

Whether a man's behaviour is difficult depends partly on the way the woman sees it. This determines how she feels about it and how she reacts to it. Sometimes it is possible to change the way you see the man's behaviour so that it ceases to cause you a problem.

This can be a hazardous route to take, however. Many men would love their partners to deal with their behaviour by changing their view of it, and some put pressure on the woman to do this. Chris and Amanda provide a clear example of this potentially destructive process. She has been persuaded that her opposition to his infidelity is based on her own personal inadequacy, and that 'spiritual growth' would cure her problem. Perhaps it would, but not while she tries to force herself to accept that which she finds unacceptable. Spiritual growth is not concerned with accepting what we may find unacceptable, but with having clearer insight into *why* we find things unacceptable. This allows us to assess whether our reaction is really a valid response to what is happening, or whether our judgement is clouded and our reaction distorted.

A new perspective must be a matter of free choice. Most of the women whose stories appear in this book have changed the way they see their relationships. The choices that these women made might be totally unacceptable to others; because one individual's way of dealing with a situation works for her, this does not imply that this is the way that other women should deal with a similar problem. What is right for one woman will not be right for everybody. The crucial point is that you make up your own mind.

Stella's relationship changed when she changed her attitude: 'I don't need him to be difficult any more, I don't want him to be difficult any more, but in the beginning, definitely. . . The way that I cope is to have a good look at why I chose a difficult man, why I perpetuate him being a difficult man, how I fit into that pattern. Because a relationship is joint, and one of you is not good and the other not bad, but it may serve your purposes to make it look that way.'

Chrissie's view of her partner's transvestism was such that it caused her no problems – perhaps rather the reverse, although outsiders saw it differently. 'I just dealt with it, like you deal with somebody stealing your clothes. It was like living with a sister sometimes! Did you borrow this?. . . I just didn't think it was much of something I had to deal with. But it wasn't until I saw other people's reactions to it that I thought, wo! what is this? It was strange, because it wasn't always just the straight people's reaction. It was my gay friends who said, isn't this a problem? And I said no, I had no problem.'

Similarly, Stella has no problem with behaviour that many women would find terrifying: 'Once I had a bruise because Tom threw something and hit me. But my father threw things and hit me, so I think my attitude to that is quite lenient. If he hit me, I would just think, what a twat, I wouldn't be interested.' Stella does not fear Tom's outbursts, nor does she fear for her own safety, so his outbursts do not cause any psychological damage.

Tessa was able to transform her view of Frank's affair so radically that instead of feeling desperately threatened by his mistress, she was able to embrace her too. 'I had this flash of inspiration that I had to let go of things. My mother couldn't let go, she was clinging to life. . . And it really made me think about the triangular situation between me, Frank and Anya. And I just felt that I had to try to dissolve this me being hurt, I had to try and be more open to Anya. So I rang her up and we spent a really nice morning together making bread and jam, and we went for a walk. And I felt OK with her. Then Frank came in and we had lunch, and after that we all went to bed together.'

But this is not a route that a woman can be pressured into taking. Had Tessa and Anya not found that they enjoyed each other's companionship on a one-to-one basis, the triangular situation could not have been resolved in this way. Nor could it have worked if Tessa had felt as Amanda does: 'Because of the frantic fear, you know, in myself. I can't bear the idea of them making love. I shut it out. It frightens me to death.'

It would be totally inappropriate for Amanda to follow Tessa's route; if she were to try to do so, it would be at the behest of her husband, not because she was following her own feelings. Tessa was very aware of the difference – as was Anya. The first time, 'It just happened, naturally. We all felt very loving towards each other. Anya and I had just opened up to each other.' On a later occasion, however, Tessa explained, 'I felt I was doing it because he'd asked me to. It felt so wrong, it was horrible. Nothing actually happened, we didn't have sex. Frank tried to have sex with Anya and she wouldn't let him, then he tried to do it with me, and I said, no way, I'm not going to. It was horrid. It wasn't spontaneous. It was Frank just trying to get his end away.'

The crucial difference was Tessa's feeling: open and loving on the first occasion; wrong on the second. Such deep feelings of rightness or wrongness should be taken seriously, never overridden.

As in Tao or Zen belief systems, the way forward does not feel hard or frightening at all, but utterly natural. When you have to struggle to find the path, it is because you cannot see the path you should be taking. Vicky recognised this: 'You can't make yourself be stronger. . . You can't force yourself.'

Changes of this sort can result from coming to see yourself and your situation from a different perspective. This was the crucial change that my therapist was able to help me with: instead of believing that I was a helpless victim of Colin's rage, I realised that I had power. Once I saw that, I was able to change the way I acted and by this means, change the whole situation.

CHAPTER 14

HOW TO AVOID BEING A VICTIM

My discovery that I could choose to stop being a victim was what led to the creation of this book. I believed that my experience proved that women in abusive relationships could, with suitable guidance, identify the features of their own behaviour that maintained their victim status. When they understood this, they could act to change the whole nature of the relationship. Listening to the women whose experiences are described here confirmed my belief.

Women do not have to be victims in relationships. It is possible to change the form of the interaction between victim and abuser so radically that neither partner plays these roles. Women can make the first moves to set this process of change in motion.

Some people find this truth unpalatable. They imagine that I am blaming the victim for her fate. In fact, I am doing nothing of the sort. I am pointing to a route out of the trap in which many such women find themselves. It is a route that I have taken, and that Vicky, in particular, describes with great clarity.

It is in the woman's interest to initiate change. In the longer term, the man is also likely to recognise that he benefits, but in the short term he is unlikely to change spontaneously. Indeed, he may find it very difficult to do so. Many abusive men are deeply apologetic after an episode of violence and promise faithfully that it will never happen again. It does happen because these men do not fully understand what is going on and they feel powerless to stop it – although of course it is possible for them to change.

Similarly, a woman is not powerless. She can stop the abuse by ceasing to allow herself to be a victim.

Standing up for yourself is the opposite of behaving like a

victim. This can be particularly difficult for women who, like me, tend to feel guilt and fear in conflict situations. This is why it is so important to get in touch with your inner strength and be clear in your own mind about what you believe and what you are aiming for.

In Part One of this book, I described how I began to understand the differences between victim behaviour and standing up for myself. The first lessons I learnt were to do with body language: that standing up for yourself is both about meeting the man's eye without flinching and about saying what you believe is right.

I came to discriminate very clearly between behaving as a victim who got abused, and seeing what I had to do to prevent abuse. In the following table I list various aspects of victim behaviour and contrast them with the behaviour of people who are less likely to be abused.

Victim behaviour	Strong woman behaviour
Victim body language	*Strong body language*
Crying, weeping, wringing hands	Keeping your face impassive, staying cool
Cringing	Standing tall
Hunching your shoulders	Straightening and relaxing your shoulders
Dropping your eyes	Looking directly at the person you're addressing
Fiddling with your hair or nails	Keeping your hands relaxed
Breathing fast and shallow	Breathing steadily and deeply
Wasting your breath	*Making your point*
Blaming yourself or him for the problem	Focusing on solutions
Pleading	Stating your position clearly
Promising to try harder next time	Addressing the real issue – like why the problem arose
Promising to do whatever he wants	Saying you'll do what you believe to be right
Struggling to persuade him when he's not interested in listening	Discussing the issue in a mutual exchange
Arguing when you know it's pointless	Offering to return to the discussion when he is willing to consider your viewpoint
Making excuses	Explaining the situation as you see it; giving reasons

Letting tension rise/raising the stakes	Tension reduction/Tactical withdrawal
Raising the volume or pitch of your voice	Speaking clearly without shouting or shrieking
Sticking around when you suspect he may attack you	Walking out if he threatens you, either verbally or with his body language
Hitting him	Refusing to take part in acts of violence
Tolerating insults or abuse	Explaining calmly that you do not tolerate abuse, and walking out when it occurs
Giving as good as you get	Refusing to resort to abuse

Lacking self-respect	Showing self-respect
Placating	Acknowledging his views and treating them with respect when appropriate
Acting defensively	Asserting your position
Feeling guilty	Feeling comfortable with yourself
Apologising when you've nothing to apologise for	Apologising only if you have behaved unreasonably or carelessly in your terms
Blaming yourself for not being perfect	Acknowledging that you can make mistakes
Lighting a cigarette	Maintaining tranquillity without drugs
Pouring yourself an alcoholic drink	Ditto

Of course, it's not possible always to be totally strong and always to act in the most appropriate way. If you demand that of yourself, you set yourself up for failure. It is enough to recognise the different patterns and consciously set out to deal with potentially threatening situations in the way that is likely to produce the best outcome for you, even if you don't feel all that strong. I found that adopting strong body language helped me to stay more cool and relaxed. When you stand tall, you feel stronger. Try it!

I shared this list with psychiatrist Bob Johnson and his wife Sue. Their comments were very illuminating. My victim behaviours, they pointed out, were the ways that children behave, whereas my strong woman behaviour was that of an adult. This made total sense to me. To stop the bullying and abuse, I had learnt to act in an adult manner.

When I act like an adult, my partner tends to respond by also acting like an adult – which means behaving in a reasonable, civilised, acceptable way. But when I acted like a frightened child, he would also behave in an immature manner. We were making each other worse by mutually triggering immature behaviour; we changed our relationship by learning to act like the mature people we actually are.

Vicky speaks of this as a crucial step in her development. 'It was almost like being a child and I was being punished. I used to say to him, why are you being mean to me? I've done nothing wrong. But I realise now I did it all badly, because I was playing up to him. . . When he came out of Rose Hill, I took on the role of mother and he was the child. Since then, we've had to work out how to be two adults. It's been quite hard.'

Vicky refers to many of the same issues as I have found to be important, for example the way she felt when she was being abused: 'I felt so ashamed of what was going on. I always thought it was my fault. . . And what I was doing was just letting him carry on, as if saying, treat me how you want. Which he did. Because he would do something to me and I would be the one to go to him, and try to get round him, rather than the other way round.

'Now I know I can't change his behaviour, but I can change *how I react* to his behaviour. And I can say this is not acceptable. You have no right to treat me like this. But the thing is, unless you really think like that, you can't say it.'

She, too, had blamed herself, felt guilty, tolerated abuse, and tried to placate her husband. Victims naturally tend to adopt passive, self-effacing roles, which make exploitation and abuse easy. Unfortunately, these are precisely the roles that girls are taught to adopt; they are characteristic of good little girls. When good girls are punished, they imagine it happens because they have failed to live up to expectations. They try harder. They seek to please. And in these ways they reward the abuser.

Vicky became aware of these patterns. 'What I call

Matthew's bad side was taking advantage of my insecure side. I was giving him the power to treat me like that.'

When she changed her behaviour, the crucial first step was to realise that he had no right to abuse her. Once she had truly recognised that, she was able to say, in a cool, adult way, that his behaviour was not acceptable. She did not go onto the offensive, attacking him or seeking to change him by persuasion or pressure; she changed her own behaviour and by this means, changed the nature of their interaction. He responded by changing the way he behaved towards her.

Louise recognises that her husband's abusive behaviour is childish: 'It was a way of forcing me to focus on him and nobody else. Just like a toddler, actually. You're talking to somebody and the toddler will pull at your shirt. If you carry on instead of dealing with it, toddlers won't leave you alone. That's how he would behave if I brushed him to one side.' Unfortunately, she seems to collude with this by taking the role of mother: 'I suppose I feel responsible for Adam to some extent... I've always had an overdeveloped sense of responsibility for other people.' Although Louise is functioning as adult, this puts Adam in the role of naughty child – which would make his behaviour more appropriate.

It is difficult to imagine Stella ever becoming a victim, except perhaps if she behaves in a childish way and provokes a fight with someone who is stronger and more ruthless than herself. However, she also sees her partner behaving sometimes 'like a child in a tantrum'. She acts to reduce the probability that this will happen: 'Before, I paid it attention; now I just ignore it. Anything about his behaviour I don't like, I just ignore.' But she recognises that she cannot afford to continue ignoring him for too long; when he persists in behaving like a child, it is likely to mean that there's something that they need to deal with. 'If I ignore it for too long, that's when he comes and shouts in my face.'

Stella admits that she can be insensitive to Tom's needs. 'I'm not now going to run my life always being attuned to somebody else's needs, I have my own.' This attitude will sometimes leave Tom feeling isolated and alone, but it will also tend to protect her from being abused or exploited. What is necessary is balance: an equal relationship between two adults, both of whom stand up for themselves.

CHAPTER 15

SETTING LIMITS

Refusing to tolerate abusive behaviour is one aspect of avoiding being a victim. But before you can stand firm against varied forms of abuse, you need to decide what is acceptable, what is tolerable, and what is not. Setting limits, and making them clear to your partner, is another crucial part of the strategy for many women who live with difficult men.

When you set limits, you cease to collude with behaviour that you find unacceptable. To do so, you have to be honest with yourself and with the man. You cannot go along with, or try to ignore, behaviour that is not acceptable to you.

What is unacceptable has to be defined in terms of your feelings, but it must also be discussed and negotiated with your partner. Obviously there are potential pitfalls. If what you define as unacceptable covers too wide a range of your partner's everyday behaviour, he may be unable or unwilling to change it and you may find that you are not living with an individual you can tolerate. But if you are too protective of his foibles and insufficiently protective of your own feelings, and you define unacceptable behaviour too narrowly, you will continue to suffer.

The concept of totally unacceptable behaviour must not be loosely interpreted or trivialised; it has to be limited to that which you cannot live with. For example, you may decide that you will not tolerate insults because they undermine your belief in yourself. But your response to an insult would not be the same as your response to violence. For instance, I stand and tell my partner, firmly but coolly, why I will not accept insults, whereas I deal with violence differently; even the threat of violence is enough to make me walk out.

To me, violence is unacceptable behaviour. Nobody should accept this sort of treatment. In western society, most women are in a position where they can refuse to put up with it. Of the three women who tell of life with violent men in this book,

Vicky and I decided to take this position. We both succeeded in stopping the violence within our relationships. I believe that Louise could also do so if she were to take the same sort of action.

I recognise that it may not always be possible for women to change the behaviour of violent men; some probably require professional help. Those who become violent under the influence of alcohol or drugs may become so insensitive that they do not respond in the same way as sober abusers. But I believe that such individuals form a small minority of the total group of abusive and violent men.

Vicky and I made up our minds that we did not deserve to be hit, ever. *Unacceptable behaviour must not be tolerated; it is unacceptable whatever the circumstances.* Also, we will not let anyone tell us what we think, how we feel, or in any other way seek to diminish our personhood. This may seem like a subtle point but it can be very important. When someone is seen as an inferior person or non-person (i.e. someone who cannot think, have her own views or develop ideas), she ceases to have equal rights. This process does not have to be overt for it to affect behaviour.

It is important, when you have decided that the nature of your relationship must change, to state your position clearly to your partner. Say firmly which aspects of his behaviour are unacceptable to you. Do not argue and do not be defensive about it, even if he suggests that you have adopted an irrational or otherwise indefensible position. It is simply a condition of your commitment to the relationship that this behaviour does not continue. You are not interested in defending or justifying it; it is something that is necessary *to you* and you will not be swayed from it.

You have to be sure, of course, that the position you've taken is what you personally truly believe. Make sure you've done all your thinking and soul-searching before you reach the point of classifying any aspect of his behaviour as totally unacceptable. Otherwise, there is a risk that he could undermine your position by argument. Once you have decided to stand firm, you are committed.

When you have made your position clear, give him the opportunity to share his views and feelings about it, and to ask you whatever questions he feels are necessary to clarify any aspects of what you have decided. You need him to consent to the change, at least in principle. If he truly understands that these are the only terms on which a relationship with you is acceptable, and if he values the relationship, he must consent.

Of course, there is the possibility that this will lead to a showdown. At this point, you will discover whether he is willing to have a relationship with you on terms that make life with him tolerable for you. You may have to enter some sort of negotiation – but you cannot afford to give ground to the degree that you accept the unacceptable.

Any sanction for unacceptable behaviour must be something you can actually carry out – for example refusing to sleep in the same bed with him, or going to stay elsewhere for a while. What you must not do is make threats that you cannot carry out. Women who do so are liable to end up being exploited. If your sanction is the threat of leaving him, you have to know that you really can do that. Inability to carry out this threat weakened Amanda's position: 'I thought, if that happens, that's it. Then when I discovered it had happened, I said, right, that's it, finished. But I couldn't do it. We are still together.' And Chris treats her with diminishing respect.

Having established the rules, the next step is to ensure that they are kept. If behaviour that you have defined as unacceptable has occurred, or you have good reason to believe that it is about to occur, you must leave. Leave the room, the bed or the house – whatever the situation requires. If you are aiming to prevent violence, it is essential that you get away from him whenever you perceive that there is a strong possibility that he may act in that way.

These principles can be applied to many different aspects of behaviour. Vicky and I used them to put a stop to violence.

Vicky described what happened after Matthew's relapse into violence: 'I thought, right you can let this beat you, or you can try and sort it out. . . I kept away from him for that night, then the next day, I said to him, "I'm disappointed in you, first for what you did, and second, because you haven't had the decency to apologise or speak to me." So he promised to talk after we'd put the bairns to bed. And he did talk. He said he was ever so sorry, it won't happen again. So I said, "I can't condone what you've done, but at least you realise you've done wrong." I believe he hadn't thought he was doing a bad thing.' Vicky's husband has not reverted; the change seems to be permanent. They have left their abusive relationship behind and replaced it with one that is far more satisfying to both partners.

I now leave the room if Colin shouts at me or insults me. I explain why I am doing so. I prepare myself by taking a couple of deep breaths and say something like this: 'You are behaving in the way that you know I will not accept. I am going out until I feel confident that we can discuss this without abuse.' This effectively prevents rows building to the point where he might start to behave in a potentially violent manner. In fact, this sort of situation is very rare now; a few years ago, it happened often.

When his demands or expectations are more than you can cope with, or unacceptable to you, you need to specify what you will accept and what you won't. This is what Tessa learnt to do: 'I had to make boundaries. I had to say what I was prepared to do and what I wasn't prepared to do, and know what I wanted, to be totally clear about what I wanted, what felt OK and what didn't. . . If I didn't want them to have sex in my bed, if I didn't want her to stay over when I wasn't here, I had to be clear about that.'

It is very important to tell the truth about what you are comfortable with. Victims tend to give in to try to keep the peace. Healthy relationships are built on honesty, and giving in to placate a man means denying your own feelings. This was one of the problems that Marian had, probably because of the way she had suffered at the hands of her father: 'I don't think I'd ever truly been open with Ted. . . For a long time I think I hadn't been facing up to who I am. That I am a normal woman and I do have those feelings.' As a result, Marian tended to be a passive participant in a relationship that often failed to meet her needs or desires.

CHAPTER 16

CAN WOMEN REALLY CHANGE MEN?

There are those who believe that men can't change, and that women should not attempt to change them. Women who believe this will not make any serious attempt to achieve change; they accept these men, or they leave them.

Louise has accepted Adam's abusive behaviour, despite her dislike of it: 'I got him to see a psychiatrist on one occasion, who said he was a psychopath. Which I agree with. I think he is. . . But really I don't think it's treatable. In fact, I now know that.' In Louise's view, trying to stop Adam from behaving in this way would be a waste of time and energy. By labelling him as an untreatable psychopath, she has absolved both him and herself of responsibility for any further action.

Believing that behaviour cannot change has a variety of important consequences:

You either have to tolerate it or give up on the relationship – both of which may be unsatisfactory solutions.

You avoid accepting any responsibility – if he can't change, then your own behaviour has no influence, therefore you don't need to look at it.

You support the man's belief that he cannot control the way he acts and thus effectively excuse his actions. In this way, you help to perpetuate patterns of behaviour that are damaging to both of you.

You remove hope that the relationship can be improved, thus increasing the probability that it will end – to the potential detriment of children and society at large.

You increase the probability of serial relationships which express the same type of dysfunction, both by failing to look at the way your behaviour might elicit dysfunctional behaviour and by failing to cure your partner's dysfunctional behaviour. Thus if you remarry, both of you could carry this dysfunction into future relationships.

You store up unresolved anger which may poison future relationships.

You model dysfunctional behaviour to your children, who may carry it into their relationships.

It is true that some men will *refuse* to change their behaviour, but this does not mean that they could not do so if they chose. Frank, Tessa's husband, will never promise sexual exclusivity: he believes that infidelity is necessary to his creativity, and insists that he has been totally consistent about this since before their marriage. Tessa reported his view: 'I would be blocking his art if I tried to stop it.' Similarly, Amanda either has to accept Chris's infidelity, or leave him. He will not voluntarily give up his mistress.

Sometimes limited change in the man's behaviour is enough to allow the relationship to continue, as it was for Tessa. Both Frank and Chris accepted limits set on their actions by their wives – in particular, that they should not have sex with their mistresses in the marital bed.

Sophie's husband refuses to acknowledge that there might be any problem with his behaviour. He is effectively refusing to consider change, so it is very difficult to see what action Sophie can take to create a satisfactory marital relationship with him. 'Every time I try to talk about this, he will say, "I don't know what you're talking about," or "I don't know what you mean," or "What problem?"'

When difficult men care enough about their partners' feelings to recognise that their behaviour creates a serious problem in the relationship, they can and do change. But they may not be able to achieve such change through their own efforts, especially if the problem is associated with deep-seated, and probably subconscious, fear. When this is at the root of violence, men are likely to feel that they cannot control their actions.

But relationship problems involve both partners, and are often products of the dynamic interaction of the partners.

Women can change the nature of the interaction by changing their behaviour unilaterally.

Vicky, once again, put this very clearly: 'I changed in those few weeks when he was away, and realised I wasn't as daft as I thought I was, and I wouldn't fall to bits every time he walked out the door. Then when he came home, he maybe wanted to act just the same, but found a different me, found somebody who wouldn't put up with everything. . . He was having to get used to my behaviour, because my behaviour had changed towards him. I say now to my friend, you can't change the way he behaves, but you can change the way you behave.'

Vicky, in common with many women who live with violent men, had been behaving in such a way that her husband was effectively rewarded for abusing her. There had not been sufficient incentive (apart from his unconvincing assertion that he did not want to frighten her) for him to change. He was behaving as he had learnt to behave when he was a boy, reacting to deep-seated fear induced by a violent father.

We learn most of our social behaviour in childhood, when we are most flexible and impressionable. But the ability to learn exists throughout our lives. Learned behaviour can always be changed.

Unfortunately, many women behave in such a way that they increase the risk that men will abuse them. The way this happens may be familiar from studies of mothers and children, but few people seem willing to extrapolate the same principles to interactions between adults – even when they are clearly behaving in infantile ways. If man is demanding attention and a woman takes no notice, he may escalate demands to such an extent that she can no longer ignore him. This may mean violence – as Louise explained when she compared her husband with a toddler. If he achieves what he wants by this means, he is rewarded for being violent, just as children will scream louder until mother gives in to their demands.

When women attempt to placate abusive men by seeking to give them what they think they want – such as sexual gratification – they are rewarding them for abusive behaviour. This sort of response is very dangerous. While it might prevent violence in the short term, it will make abuse more frequent in the longer term.

Family therapists teach mothers of difficult children that they must refuse to give in to the child's demands when it screams, but instead listen more readily when the child speaks normally. Then, the child is rewarded for speaking normally rather than screaming. Women can use the same principle to manage some types of difficult men.

It's *behaviour* that matters – not intentions, words, threats or promises. Women can learn to manage situations that previously seemed out of control by consistently behaving in a way that is deliberately designed to reduce or prevent problems. This is what Vicky and I did to stop our partners' abuse. This sort of approach can transform relationships.

Consistency is crucial. If your partner is abusive, you have to be totally determined and totally consistent. *Never* say you'll walk out, allow yourself to be persuaded to stay, and tolerate a return to abuse. If he's abusive when you return, you have to leave again *immediately*. The message must be very clear: if he abuses you, you leave. You do not tolerate abuse.

At the same time, you need to ensure that the underlying motivation for the abuse is addressed. This may be something that you work on with a counsellor or psychotherapist, but you can make progress without such help by building up the positive features of your relationship. You can extend the principles of behaviour therapy by selectively rewarding loving, reasonable and co-operative behaviour. Rewards can be anything from smiles and cuddles to compliments and gifts.

Most of the use of rewards in relationships is unconscious; we do it without being aware of it. To change a partner's behaviour and change a relationship, it may be necessary to become more aware of the pattern of rewards. When you change your own behaviour, you can choose to reward desirable behaviour by responding to it in a positive way, and cease to reward undesirable behaviour, perhaps by making your objections clear and withdrawing. Punishment – whether physical or emotional – should not be used. The aim is to remove this from the relationship because its effects are destructive and dangerous.

If you can modify the timing of rewards, you can change behaviour. It's as simple as that.

CHAPTER 17

SHARING THE PAIN

What do women – young women, anyway – discuss with their closest friends more than any other single thing? Men. The men they care about, the men with whom they share their lives, the men who alternately delight and madden them. Women's magazines are full of articles about them; agony columns are devoted to the problems they cause. Talking about relationships is very important to women.

But women who live with difficult men often feel they can't talk about their partners' most distressing features. I was astonished at how often the women I interviewed told me that nobody knew what had been going on in their homes. Most had tried to raise the subject with their closest female friends or family members, but they had not continued for long. Talking about the problems of living with a difficult man is not encouraged. The worse the problem, it seemed, the more probable it was that women could not share their experience.

I don't believe that this is because it's an especially distressing topic of conversation. We can discuss other painful issues, like illness or difficult relatives. We'll be offered sympathy, maybe even practical help. If we're with close family or caring friends, most of us can talk through our distress for as long as it takes. We get the full support of the female community when we ask for help with these sorts of problem.

But tell your sister or your best friend about the outrage perpetrated on you day after day by your husband or partner, and she will turn away, saying 'I don't know why you stay with him', or something similar. End of subject. You learn pretty quickly that you are a fool to be in this situation and you deserve no sympathy.

Here's Amanda's voice: 'I would like to be able to share this with people, but I can't tell anybody, really. Whoever I tell, they can't believe that I'm still there. . . It's not empowering to me, when people say I should leave him.'

And Tessa's: 'I started telling friends but they weren't any help. They'd all look at me and say, "You're out of your brain! Tell him to fuck off!" But it's not that easy. As you know!. . . It's bloody unhelpful. I just stopped talking to anybody.'

And here is Vicky: 'I felt really alone. I had my family, but I didn't feel I could go to them. Everybody said to me, everyone I spoke to, oh, get rid of him, divorce him straight away, but the thing is, a lot of the time it's not easy to do that. Sometimes it's harder to walk away, specially when you've got a low self-esteem, which I did have. . . There's also the children to think of.'

Chrissie told one friend: 'The only person I told thought I had been really stupid. But I couldn't share this with people – it could be very damaging to him. Smack is still the big no-no drug. . . It does have a huge stigma.'

Sophie is unusual in talking about her relationship. But the response is the same: 'Everybody who knows me says, get rid of him! Send him down the road!'

I learnt to avoid talking about what went on between Colin and me, although I believe many of my friends had a good idea what was happening. I too found it very unhelpful when people told me I should leave him. They weren't acknowledging that the relationship was multi-dimensional, and that I still loved him.

Simplistic answers just don't help. Women who live with difficult men do want to share the pain; they long for the support of their sisters and friends, but they rarely get it. They get glib brush-offs.

Many women sense that this would be the reaction they'd meet, so they don't say anything in the first place. They don't want to mention something that's stigmatised, like the fact that their husband can be violent, or abuses drugs or alcohol. They know that they will not get the nurturing hug, the warmth that they need to soothe the pain.

Social taboos, assumptions, and rules about acceptable and unacceptable behaviour have a bearing on this. There are two acceptable scenarios: happy relationships, to which we aspire, and failed relationships, which we may leave without stigma. The middle ground between these extremes is dangerous, particularly if the man's behaviour comes into a category deemed 'unacceptable' by our society – which includes violence, addiction and infidelity.

In such situations, our culture's remedy is for the woman to leave. If she refuses to do so, she threatens the social consensus and thus becomes dangerous. Women who find themselves too close to these boundaries of social acceptability become intuitively aware that they must keep their experience secret.

The emotion we feel is shame. We are ashamed of being caught in this trap, we do not want other people to know: it is a sign of personal failure. Louise makes this clear: 'Some of the worst moments for me have been when it's been in public, and I've known that if I didn't get away quickly, he'd actually thump me in public. Once it was at a garden party in the village. I could see from the thunderous look on his face that something was building, and I was just desperately frightened. But I couldn't stay where I was because I knew it would happen in front of everybody.'

It makes no difference whether the woman is to blame or not: the situation itself is taboo. But anyway, most women do feel that they are to some degree responsible for allowing the situation to come about. While women who are bullied and beaten do feel unfairly treated, many still imagine that if they were better wives, their husbands would not pick on them so often.

This is part of what women learn from the abuser in these situations: he tells her that she's to blame for her fate, and while part of her mind screams that it's not fair, she doesn't deserve this, another part internalises and absorbs the message. He says he's angry because she has failed. Never mind that he doesn't have the right to treat her this way. He points to the flaw in her character and she accepts that it is there.

So we react by feeling ashamed. On top of that, most women don't want to bring their friends' and families' approbation onto the head of their partners. They don't want him to be publicly shamed. After all, this is the man with whom they choose to stay. They want to hang onto whatever pride they can.

As a result, the burden of living with a difficult man is one that each woman carries alone. And this means that we are unable to learn from each other about coping strategies. Vicky, once again, is the exception. She was already clarifying her coping strategy so that she could help a friend whose husband abused her. But it was because she had felt so alone that she wanted to contribute to this book.

Nevertheless, friends can be a lifeline for women who live with difficult men. They can offer cuddles, shoulders to cry on, sanctuary when necessary. If you have a friend who is going through this sort of pain, listen to her, sympathise, and help her to stay in touch with her own sense of self. Help her with practical solutions. Help her plan effective strategies for dealing with the problem.

If you can, offer her a place to stay if she wants or needs to get away. It's not helpful if all you do is to tell her to leave the man. You can be sure she will have given that a lot of thought. She will not leave unless and until she feels ready to do so.

CHAPTER 18

PROFESSIONAL HELP

For each of the women in this book who succeeded in making dramatic changes in their relationships with difficult men, professional help played an important part. Counsellors, psychotherapists and psychiatrists all figure in their stories. They offer the non-judgemental support and insight which most people need during the period of transition when they are working on a difficult relationship.

I doubt if I would have been able to stop Colin's abuse without a period of therapy. This was what opened my eyes to the way my behaviour allowed the abuse to continue, and what I could do to prevent it. It was through therapy that I was able to understand and relinquish my inappropriate childish reactions to my partner's threatening behaviour, and find the courage to stand up to him as an adult.

In addition, therapy helped me to talk through the issues around the problems in our relationship. It made me aware of aspects that I had never thought of, and probably would never have recognised without the wisdom and gentle guidance of my counsellor. I was able to bring this understanding home to my partner, so that he too could understand what was going on. As he came to understand more, he blamed me less; his attitudes also began to change.

He has always said he wanted an equal relationship with me; he didn't want me to be afraid of him. But he did not fully realise how afraid abuse made me. I believe he was reluctant to acknowledge this – partly because he didn't feel he could control it. For me, explaining how I felt, and why I felt the way I did, was an important step towards healing the rifts in our relationship. I am not sure that I would have been able to do this without counselling.

For many years, I had wanted him to go for help because I believed that our problem was primarily his problem. He refused. But in the end, it was enough for me to raise the issues that came up in my therapy, and to make conscious changes in my behaviour. This in turn led to changes in the way he treated me.

Vicky and her husband had professional help, together and separately. She found it valuable both as an aid to communication between herself and her husband, and to build her faith in herself. 'In the end, what the psychiatrist said to him was that he put up this wall between us. And I'm knocking, saying, "Let me in, let me in." One day, the psychiatrist said, your wife will stop knocking and she'll walk away.' Later, Vicky was referred to a bereavement counsellor, who helped her to focus on her own needs and desires: 'She'd say, what do you want? Don't tell me what he wants, what do you want?' Vicky's counsellor had her practise making daily decisions and thinking for herself.

Tessa also spoke very highly of her counsellor: 'I started seeing this brilliant counsellor. She's really professional and so clear. She never said leave him, she never said he's a bastard. A couple of times I could see her professional thing slipping, but she never ever judged. She said, you've just been through so much and you handled it so well. And I said I couldn't have managed without her. . . I've only seen her about eight times but it's been enough.' Tessa's counsellor helped her to set limits to what she would and would not accept, and to understand that she did have the right to decide what she would tolerate in her own home.

Professional help does not seem to have been so effective for those men who tried it, however. Only Vicky's husband recognised – after his dramatic breakdown – that he needed help and persisted with it. This may be because the others were unwilling to acknowledge that there was any problem with them. Louise's husband's visit to a psychiatrist proved fruitless: 'I got him to see a psychiatrist on one occasion, who said he was a psychopath. Which I agree with: I think he is. None of which made any difference.'

For counselling or psychotherapy to be effective, the client has to want to participate and be willing to change. Consent is absolutely crucial. For this reason, pushing an unwilling partner to see a therapist is usually pointless: he is likely to block potential progress.

Psychotherapy can teach men to stop being violent, as Bob Johnson has proved through his work with prisoners at Parkhurst. However, he emphasises the need for consent. He succeeds because he gains the trust of these men and gets their full consent before starting the potentially dangerous process of uncovering and neutralising the repressed causes of their violent behaviour.

Over the course of my life, and years of problems with both Colin and my previous husband, I spent many hours with counsellors and therapists of various kinds. Most of them, frankly, achieved nothing. Only Charleen Agostini, whose approach was based on psychosynthesis, was truly effective. My experience suggests that professionals vary enormously; one may succeed where others fail. It is important neither to blame yourself nor to give up on therapy if your particular therapist seems unable to help you. Shop around – there's plenty of choice.

To find professional help that works for you, you need to be selective. These are my suggestions on choosing a therapist:

Trust your intuition. You need to feel you can trust your therapist totally. If you are not sure about this by the third session, look for someone else.

Go for interactive therapy – not someone who simply listens, nods occasionally, or only repeats what you have said back to you. More directive therapies work better.

Look for real improvements in the way you feel. These should be obvious by the end of the third session. You may have temporary downswings – because you're likely to be dealing with painful memories and distressing issues – but you should be aware of deeper improvement. If this is not apparent, look for someone else.

You should be discovering not only why you feel the way you do, but how you can feel different. It's not just a matter of uncovering the past but also of moving forward. Positive solutions are necessary.

Cost is no guide to potential effectiveness. Most therapists will charge something, but paying more will not ensure greater effectiveness.

If the therapist tells you that you may have to continue seeing her or him for years, go elsewhere. There is no evidence that lengthy forms of treatment such as analysis are any more helpful than shorter interventions. In fact, the reverse may be true.

Finding a therapist or counsellor is necessarily something of a hit-or-miss process. Your friends or your doctor may be able to recommend somebody. You may have met a counsellor socially – Charleen was a friend before she became my therapist. If you have a particular interest in a specific system of therapy, you can seek a local practitioner. Or you can contact an organisation such as Relate.

Your doctor may be willing to refer you for counselling or psychotherapy on the NHS. Many practices now employ a counsellor. But do remember, just because you have been referred to a particular individual, that doesn't mean that individual is the right person to help you. If the treatment isn't working, return to your GP and ask if you can be transferred to somebody else.

Similarly, if you are seeing a Relate counsellor and you are not making progress, ask if you can see someone different. You will probably have to wait, but there's no point trying to work with a counsellor with whom you feel uncomfortable.

PART FIVE

THE CONTEXT

CHAPTER 19

CULTURE AND THE STATUS QUO

To understand what is going on in relationships, it is important to recognise the part played by larger forces in society.

In some parts of India, according to a recent report in *The Lancet*, the majority of women suffer regular beatings at the hands of their husbands.* Domestic violence is seen as normal, justified, and acceptable. Women in such a culture would not consider an abusive husband difficult. They might be ashamed at getting beaten, but because it meant they had failed in their duty as wives, not because violence is seen as wrong.

Britain is very different. Women are encouraged to show zero tolerance of domestic violence – to leave at the first blow. Men who hit their wives are despised. The media expressed total outrage when it became known that Gazza (footballer Paul Gascoigne) had thumped his wife and suggested that despite his talent, he should be excluded from the English football team because of it. Nevertheless, abuse is prevalent and victims feel so ashamed that few will admit to their experience.

Cultures also differ in their views on male sexual fidelity. The French are said to be much more relaxed about this than the British; certainly their media show far less prurient interest. Where a British woman is likely to feel very threatened, her French counterpart might shrug it off.

Culture affects both the probability that a man will behave in a way that his wife or partner finds unacceptable, and her perception of his behaviour. In addition, it determines the reaction to the situation both by society at large and by individuals close to the couple.

* [Jejeebhoy SJ and Cook RJ, *State accountability for wife-beating: the Indian challenge*] *The Lancet*, vol 349, March 1997

Human society has been moving steadily towards individualism. Tribal groups subdivided into extended families, which in turn have subdivided into nuclear families. Now, the minimal unit of the couple is under stress, with more people choosing to live alone than ever before. For many people, the social and economic benefits of group living no longer outweigh the disadvantages of dealing with other selfish individuals on a day-to-day basis.

At the same time, our culture has become more competitive. Over the last few decades, we have witnessed the growth of human scrap-heaps – sink estates populated by single mothers, neglected elderly people, rampaging addicts, youth with no stake in society. In contrast, the ranks of the super-rich grow. Personal worth is measured solely in economic terms. This is a culture which fosters antagonism and self-centred behaviour, where violence is becoming more prevalent, more pervasive. And as men become increasingly insecure, they tend to become more abusive. Larger numbers turn to drink and drugs and more become depressed. Among the excluded underclass, it is almost inevitable that behaviour will revert to more primitive patterns since, as 'civilised' society withdraws, this is what remains.

The women who live with these men suffer the effects of damaging social forces, particularly the resurgence of more primitive social behaviour. Male dominance is inherent in primate societies. Despite our civilisation, we still have primate brains. Dominant males get the most breeding opportunities. Sex and dominance are the twin themes of problems with men.

Morality is the construct created by human civilisation to control primitive and antisocial behaviour. For more than a thousand years in Britain, the expression of male sexual opportunism and dominance has been directed and controlled by reference to a higher authority – God. By purporting to speak on behalf of God, religion became the moral authority to which everyone deferred. Religious institutions defined the nature of relationships between men and women, and its dictates were seen as more important than any desires that individuals might express.

The bonds between a couple were dependent less on their personal ethics than on the rules of their religion, and disputes between individuals could usually be resolved by reference to the teachings of their religion. However, most religions support male dominance; this was built into the marriage vows. Women, bowing to this higher authority, accepted their inferior role.

Over the last century, civil authority has come to replace that of religious institutions. But the State, having no moral authority, reaches as deeply into individual lives and relationships. Although it is often based on religious beliefs, these precepts are distorted by second-hand delivery.

With the weakening of external authority, the particular contract between individual partners in marriage and similar long-term relationships now bears the burden of defining the roles of the partners. The contract is not 'given': it has to be negotiated and accepted. The full implications of this change are rarely recognised; many people enter partnerships which are intended to be lifelong without discussing the nature and limits of the relationship or the implicit contract that both partners accept.

This contract is largely assumed and rarely fixed or recorded, but it is nevertheless influential. It carries a range of rights and responsibilities which partners may wish to renegotiate at any time. In theory, it is based on mutual acceptance and agreement in the context of shared ethics – but this theoretical equality is often distorted in practice by the effects of male dominance and female passive acceptance. The male may try to impose his view of reality, or his interests, on the female. And often, she will accept a position of less power in the relationship.

By accepting an inferior position, she becomes vulnerable to abuse. In India, male violence is clearly linked with acknowledged and explicit inequality. In Britain, it is more likely to be associated with implicit inequality. Some of this inequality is due to the way innate differences between men and women can create imbalance in the interaction between them, but much is due to assumptions drawn from our culture and carried, unquestioned and unrecognised, into our relationships. This is the mental baggage we bring with us; all of us smuggle in things of which we are unaware.

Women bring different values to the culture from men. As mothers and carers, women cannot be entirely selfish – the race would not survive if this were the case. Women are group creatures who place a high value on co-operation. Problems arise when a co-operative individual, who will tend to bow to the consensus of the group, is paired with a competitive individual who works by attempting to get the group to agree with him. Unless women are aware of this clash of dynamics, they may find themselves trying to maintain consensus by constantly giving in to pressure from men. This will perpetuate imbalance and increase inequality.

The influence of feminism has failed to strengthen female values. It has not been fashionable for women to define and accentuate the female. To a large degree, the struggle for equality led women to adopt male patterns of behaviour, thus allowing antisocial forces to become stronger. Women cannot become 'good men'; they need to focus on becoming strong women, true to their own nature and values.

Women can do this by asserting their equality – not just on a personal level, but also on a cultural level. By this, I mean asserting the equal, although different, importance of values that predominate among women. Co-operation and community are such values, and they are crucial to social relationships. When they become weak, societies degenerate into conflict. The female, caring values are not weaknesses: they are essential to human happiness and social harmony. When women realise their strength and speak truthfully, without apology, about the importance of these issues, they are respected.

Many men refuse to think deeply about issues of this sort. They benefit from relationships with women but fail to take responsibility for sustaining them. It is a well-documented fact that men who lose their wives suffer more severely than women who lose their husbands; yet because ensuring the smooth functioning of social relationships is a female, more than a male, concern, men will tend not to be as active as women in nurturing their marriages. They rarely acknowledge just how important this is, and they are often reluctant to put the necessary energy and commitment into solving interpersonal problems. Women are much more likely than men to notice that such problems are developing and to seek ways of solving them.

Women also need to assert the importance of their values for the sake of successive generations. We do not want our daughters to be bullied, our sons to become violent. We have both the power and the responsibility to change the society in which we live.

Women need, most of all, to take a stand against male dominance and the values associated with it. We cannot afford to allow ourselves to be shouted down. But neither can we afford to try to take on men on their own terms, by playing their competitive games. It is the male culture that we must change.

Although culture creates the patterns of behaviour that cause such misery and tension within relationships, women also collude with them. We choose dominant men because we see them as sexy and exciting – but these are precisely the men who are most likely to cause us problems later. Then we feed the very vices we abhor. We suck up to bullies, placate abusers, try to make ourselves desirable to philanderers. Almost every woman in this book recognised that the features that attracted her to the man were very closely linked to those that could make her life a misery.

The conclusion has to be that we like these features of masculinity – so long as they are kept within strict limits. But the only person who can create those limits and persuade a man to stick to them is the woman he loves. Men are impossible. We just have to do the best we can with them.

CHAPTER 20

TAKING RESPONSIBILITY

The only way an individual woman can achieve change, whether in her home or in the wider culture, is by taking personal responsibility for that change. I have been attacked for doing this on the grounds that this frees the difficult man from his responsibility for the problems he causes. I reject the criticism because it is self-defeating: I could continue telling him to change his ways till I was hoarse, and nothing would improve.

I also reject this criticism because I know – both from my own experience and from the experience of other women – that blaming the man alone for a problem that arises in a relationship is rarely justified. While I acknowledge that this varies from problem to problem (addiction, in particular, may be an individual problem), the woman's behaviour does affect the situation. Blaming another person is opting out. It confirms your role as a victim rather than an active player in a relationship. This can only add to the damage.

The dogmatic approach which says that women's sole responsibility in this situation, is to leave men who behave badly, doesn't work. It doesn't work for individual women and it doesn't work for society. In fact, this approach – for all that it is touted as serving women's interests – perpetuates the culture which is the bedrock of those features we dislike.

The belief that men cannot stop being violent is the worst aspect of this dogma. It means that attempts to teach them non-violent ways of handling conflict tend to be blocked. This was precisely Bob Johnson's experience when he showed that he could cure psychopaths in Parkhurst prison: the prison service disbanded the unit where he worked, moved the men with whom he was working to other prisons, and prevented him from contacting them.

The people who denied my experience in ending my partner's violence towards me, and who tried to prevent this message from being treated as credible, were behaving in a similar way. Indeed, so consistent is our cultural reaction to violent men – throw them out, throw them in prison and throw away the key (except in time of war, when they are transformed from monsters into heroes) – that one must wonder what motivates it. Is it, in fact, a way of maintaining the status quo in our society?

Our culture reached its dominance in the world at large, when much of the world was part of the British Empire, through violence and aggression. Perhaps the underlying problem here is that the culture actually values aggression, just as individual women value dominant men. Women, who can determine the nature of the culture as much as men, must take responsibility for promoting awareness that aggression and competitive styles of relating to one another are fundamentally antisocial and should be replaced with co-operation. We can do this in our homes and social networks, through our work, and by making our voices heard through the media. Culture is that which is repeated. If we repeat our views sufficiently often, the culture will change.

The underlying problem is linked with the perceived inequality of the sexes. Part of the answer is to achieve greater equality. But asking someone to let you be equal does not work: you have to get up off your knees and assert your equality. This is why it is so important that women should value themselves – not just as mothers and home-makers, but as independent individuals.

Some people may feel that I am pushing at an open door, that men and women are already equal in our society. I would answer that they are not: that the prevalence of domestic violence and abuse of women reflects continuing inequality. In many women's relationships with difficult men there is obvious inequality, and progress towards resolving the problems means increasing equality within the relationship.

The exceptions in this book were Chrissie's relationship with an addict and Sophie's relationship with a deeply disturbed man. In each of these cases, the man's personal problems are apparent, and the woman's main task – if she wants to stay in the relationship – is to find a way of surviving despite them, if she cannot help him to resolve them. But even in these cases, the woman's sense of her own value is crucial; this is what gives her the strength to deal with the situation.

So the key aspect of the woman's responsibility is actually her responsibility to herself. Whether or not she is able to resolve the problem by showing her partner that she will not tolerate unacceptable behaviour, her first concern has to be her own feelings and needs. Taking responsibility for dealing with the problem does not mean adjusting to her difficult partner's demands. It implies the reverse.

The mistake that women tend to make with difficult men is that they try to cope through self-sacrifice. But effective and constructive answers do not require sacrifice. They require personal development. They require that we behave as strong adults, not good girls. They require that we stand up for ourselves and refuse to tolerate unacceptable behaviour. They require that we stop getting bogged down in ineffective ways of thinking such as, 'it's not fair', and instead focus our energy on solving our problems.

When women act purposefully, positively and consistently for themselves they can transform their relationships. And then the men won't be so difficult after all.

Addresses for further help

The British Association for Counselling, 1 Regent Place, Rugby, Warwickshire. Tel: 01788 550 899. A central organisation which provides information about individuals and organisations who offer counselling.

Marriage Care, 1 Blythe Mews, Blythe Road, London W14 0NW. Tel: 0171 371 1341. An advisory service offering support to couples where one or both partners are Catholic.

Relate, The address and telephone number of your local Relate centre can be found in the telephone directory. A telephone enquiry will provide information about the centre's counselling services, and can be used to arrange an initial appointment.

The Samaritans offer telephone and befriending help to people who feel desperate. Their local address and phone number will be in your telephone directory. Available 24 hours every day of the year.

More books from Vermilion

The Relate Guide to Better Relationships by Sarah Litvinoff.
For couples starting their relationship or wanting to improve it.

The Relate Guide to Starting Again by Sarah Litvinoff.
For couples who are divorcing or divorced.

The Courage to Heal by Ellen Bass and Laura Davis.
A self-help book for women who were sexually abused during childhood.

Families and How to Survive Them by John Cleese and Robin Skynner.
A light-hearted but extremely informative look at how our families make
us who we are.

These and other Vermilion books are available by telephoning
the TBS order line on: 01206 255 800